ACKNOWLEDGEMENTS

I WOULD LIKE TO say a thank you to:

Donna Morris and family for info and
photographs of The Dutch Café;
Bernie and Mike Byrne,
Nigel and Debbie Greenberg,
Bill Heckle, The Cavern.
The Quarrymen; Rod, Colin, Len,
Duff Lowe, Nigel and Chas.
Major Longmore, Salvation Army.
Stephen Guy and staff, Lowlands.
Liverpool Record Office.
Liverpool Daily Post and Echo.
Sue Garry.
Thelma Grant.
David Bedford.
George Astbury.

To my wife Sandy:
My son Stephen and daughter-in-law Linda; James our
grandson and our friends in New York, Jennie and Lou
Longobardi, and Linda and Jimmy Beggs for all their
support.

FOREWORD
Bill Heckle

MY EARLIEST MEMORIES of Quarry Bank were as a schoolboy football player enjoying twice yearly 'blood baths' against our local school rivals. As a Beatles fan, I was always fascinated by the fact that my idols, The Beatles, had their roots firmly entrenched in that school, whereas our biggest boast as a pupil at The Holt was that it was Ken Dodd's old school. I suppose we lost that one!

Fast forward to 1997 and the 40th Anniversary of The Cavern Club and, as co-owner, I was thrilled that the invitations to five of the original Quarrymen to attend our celebration had been gratefully accepted. I was later astounded to find out that they had not been in the same room together for nearly 40 years. I was further shocked when they all decided to get on stage together and perform late that afternoon.

Furthermore, they all enjoyed it so much that they decided to re-form and go on tour! WOW!

Fast forward again; September 2017 and I was privileged to be invited to spend some time with Paul McCartney in Brooklyn, prior to his performance. And guess what? All he talked about was The Quarrymen and, in particular, how he keeps looking back at his amazing life and can't help thinking about how his life changed and was eternally shaped, the day he was introduced by Ivan Vaughan to a certain John Lennon!! Well as they say, 'The story starts here'.

Bill Heckle.
Director, Cavern City Tours, January 2018.

CHAPTERS

THE QUARRYMEN
1956 - 1959

22nd June 1957: L to R: Colin Hanton, Eric Griffiths, John Lennon, Len Garry, Pete Shotton and Rod Davis

THE QUARRYMEN, JOHN Lennon's first group, was formed at Quarry Bank High School for Boys, in the Liverpool suburb of Allerton, sometime during the summer of 1956.

The lineup consisted of Quarry Bank pupils John Lennon (guitar), Pete Shotton (washboard), Bill Smith (tea-chest bass), Eric Griffiths (guitar) and Rod Davis (banjo). There were also a couple of friends, Ivan Vaughan and Nigel Walley and ultimately by 1957, Len Garry, permanently taking over on tea-chest bass. Colin

Dear Charlie,

John and I started our incredible friendship in 1946 when we both started school at Mosspits Lane. John a year older than myself was in a different class. John was noted for his disruptive behaviour in class and Mimi his aunty moved him to Dovedale Primary. We use to meet up in the evenings as John lived down the road to me and we continued to get up to schooboy pranks. At the age of 11 years I moved onto Liverpool Bluecoat School and John to Quarry Bank.

I was more interested in Sport than academics and I was to become a Golf Professional in later life. John on the other hand was more interested in music so that was where his future laid.

I left school at 15 at the same time Quarry Men were formed, I became a part time Tea Chest player but John felt my services would best be served if I was to take the role of Manager, being that I had started my training at Lee Park Golf Club and I mixed with influential people we thought that this would enable the group to get worthwhile bookings and become better known.

At that time Alan Sytner had just opened the Cavern and was looking for some class acts so I stepped in and arranged for the Quarry Men to give an audition at the Club. It went well for us to get our first appearance at the Cavern the rest is history.

Over the years we kept in touch as you have probably seen the iconic picture of John and myself at 17 walking down Lime Street and from time to time I visited his house in Weybridge on several occasions.

I myself became a Golf Pro and was attached to several clubs in England before ending my career as Golf Director of Lima Golf Club in Peru.

John was a good friend, he showed his talents as an artist and of course his talent as a world class musician.

Kind Regards.

Letter from Nigel Walley, The Quarrymen's manager

Hanton, a Woolton friend of Eric's, who was a bit older and already an apprenticed upholsterer, agreed to join the group as their drummer.

While their first performance was actually at a school dance in November 1956, John Lennon would erroneously remember their first as a gig that took place over six months later, on the back of a lorry, in Rosebery Street, Toxteth, Liverpool 8, on 22nd June, 1957.

"Our first appearance was in Rosebery Street - it was their Empire Day celebrations. They had this party out in the street. We played from the back of a lorry."

John Lennon, Anthology

John's memory of that performance was likely influenced by the fact that the Rosebery Street gig also happened to be the first time the group was photographed in action. It was also a celebration for Liverpool's 750th birthday, as opposed to Empire Day. The photo was taken by me Charles Roberts, a friend of Colin's, who lived in Rosebery Street and witnessed the festivities that day.

But the original Quarrymen lineup wasn't to last very long. In fact, by early 1958, only John and Colin remained from the group who performed in Rosebery Street, though, by then, Paul McCartney and George Harrison had now joined. Pete Shotton, who was and would remain John's best mate for life, left the group in

Pete Shotten, Billy Turner, John Lennon and Len Garry larking around

Bill Smith, Pete Shotton, John Lennon, Eric Griffiths and Rod Davis at Quarry Bank School

late 1957, as did Rod Davis shortly after the arrival of Paul McCartney. As a banjoist, he really preferred folk and jazz to the rock 'n' roll direction that John and Paul now favoured for the fledgling group. Rod, who was also a very good scholar, left to continue his education at the prestigious Cambridge University and spent his career in academia and tourism, though he did manage to appear on a record in 1961 with a group called the Trad Grads.

Founder member Eric Griffiths quit when George Harrison was recruited at the end of 1957. Eric joined the Merchant Navy as a cadet. After a short career on the high seas, he joined the Prison Service and lived in Scotland for many years.

Len Garry, who, like John, fancied himself as Elvis, and had a great singing voice to go along with that dream, last played the tea-chest with the group in late 1957 and, after suffering from an extended illness that began in August 1958, never did

Len Garry

Colin Hanton

return to his role in the group. Len went on to a successful career as an architect.

Colin Hanton would drum alongside John, Paul & George (occasionally joined by piano player, John Duff Lowe) until early 1959, including on their first record. But, after a post-gig argument with Paul McCartney, Colin quit the group, gave up the drums, put them away in the cupboard indefinitely, and settled into a successful and satisfying career as an upholsterer. Despite its bitter ending, Colin's two-year tenure in The Quarrymen would still serve as a life-changing event for him.

However, it wasn't only a significant event for Colin, but for me as well. You see, Colin and I had been friends even prior to his joining the Quarrymen. And through that friendship, I too was welcomed into the group's circle. By being so close, I shared friendships, memories

A young me in Rosebery Street

and adventures with The Quarrymen. But it wouldn't end there. I found myself in the fortunate position of becoming a contributor to Beatles history.

You see, it was I, Charlie Roberts, who was the local lad on Rosebery Street that day way back in 1957, who snapped those first photos of The Quarrymen playing.

THE BEST OF CELLARS
Oh! Darling

Entrance to the Cavern

THIS "PERSONAL INVOLVEMENT" in the Merseyside musical scene, also led to other major events in my life.

I met Sandy, my future wife, in the Cavern in 1958 (I used to tell people that it was quite dark and that I was drunk, and I did not realise what I was doing. I don't mention that anymore because I can no longer stand the repercussions!)

Sandy and I married in September 1961 and from then on finances were very difficult, as I was working lots of overtime to make ends meet. Sandy also worked long hours and on many occasions we saw little of each other, we were like ships that passed in the night. Our only child, Stephen, arrived and it was then that I realized my times with the lads were over, although we were still in touch now and again.

The original Quarrymen lived in Woolton, except Len who lived in nearby Wavertree. Where I lived in Toxteth, Liverpool 8, was a distance away across town, a geographical outsider. But The Quarrymen had always made me feel welcome as part of their gang. From the early '60s, for various reasons, we slowly lost regular touch with each other.

Both Sandy and I developed long-term health issues, but we managed to carry on working until retirement. We are still married and we are heading for our 60th wedding anniversary (in 2021) and we have lived in Woolton for the last 30 years.

Looking back now at the birth of the Quarrymen, I realize how fortunate I was to have been part of the gang. Sadly, Eric and Pete have passed on, as well as John and George. But Sandy and I still see Len, Colin, Rod and their spouses socially. At the time, we were all just normal teenagers growing up in Liverpool. None of us knew what the future was going to hold, especially for John, Paul and George.

This is my story of those early days; the days of innocence when I was there watching the group practice, going to the early gigs with them, and sometimes just larking about. There were three main interests for all of us; rock 'n' roll, girls and drink, probably in that order.

There are a lot of inaccurate stories about the early years of The Quarrymen, and most of what you read is usually taken from other exaggerated stories of that distant past, told by people who were not there. Accounts vary and with the passing of time, some

Click here to visit The Quarrymen website

stories have become more and more magnified. If you are ever in doubt, then I suggest that you contact Rod Davis on the Quarrymen website. If Rod can't give you an answer, then nobody can. As Eric used to say; "Rod knows everything", and that is certainly true when it comes to The Quarrymen, after all he was an original Quarryman!

My memory was never that good, but when I get talking to the lads, I start to remember little things long forgotten.

Older Scousers nearly all claim to have known The Quarrymen and then The Beatles. In fact, what most of them mean is that they have seen them on many occasions in the past, at the Cavern and local clubs, and they all have a story or two to tell, albeit fact or fiction.

Much has been written over the years about The Quarrymen and the Beatles, and a lot of it is imaginative, to say the least! In this book, it is not my intention to revisit stories that have been told many times before, except on occasions, to set the record straight.

I will tell you of events that have stuck in my memory for over 60 years and have not been previously recorded. They are not hearsay or exaggerated tales, but first-hand accounts of my teenage years as a friend of John Lennon and his first group, The Quarrymen.

IN MY LIFE
1939

I N 1939 DURING the early part of World War II, when Liverpool was being heavily bombed by the Luftwaffe, my mother was evacuated to Squires Gate in Blackpool where I was born on 5th October.

Liverpool bomb damage 1941, in the background is the world famous Royal Liver Building.

We returned home to Liverpool a few weeks later and, fortunately, our house at 84, Rosebery Street, was still standing, although many others in the area of Liverpool 8 had been razed to the ground.

Being so young with all of this going on around me, I knew nothing about the war, and it was only as I grew older that I became aware of what had happened in those dark times. The debris and damaged buildings surrounded the concrete bomb shelters that had been erected in most streets and, although we were warned not to, as it could be very dangerous, we climbed in and around the bombed buildings for hours on end.

In our early years, we saw the tumbled-down buildings as our playground, like another world: strange and eerie, whilst oblivious to the danger that we were in. The devastation remained for many years, a sad reminder of what had gone before, and rebuilding Liverpool was a mammoth task that took decades to accomplish.

Risen from the ashes, Liverpool is now a magnificent city that draws millions of visitors from around the world, many who return time and again.

Those who visit for the first time to experience The Beatles history and their legacy, are always amazed at the quality of the architecture, the UNESCO World Heritage Mersey waterfront, the football teams, the museums, the leafy parks and suburbs and, above all,

'Scousers', our greatest ambassadors; the people of Liverpool.

Post War

After the war, the working classes never had much money and times were very hard for many years. Not only were finances difficult, but rationing was introduced and many everyday items became impossible to buy in quantity.

Even newspapers were limited because of the shortage of newsprint. When the local chip shops were short of paper to wrap the fish and chips in, they would give a free portion of chips in exchange for old newspapers. Of course, we were always on the lookout for any discarded papers, but such was the demand, we never really found many. Only essential goods could be bought; sweets and other such luxuries were in short supply, while toys, if available, would be far too expensive.

On dark winter nights, we would walk into Liverpool City Centre and peer into the remaining brightly lit shop windows displaying the numerous unaffordable goods. On the way back home we would talk excitedly about what we had seen and what we would like. Our only hope was to wait for Father Christmas and see if he had left us anything.

I still remember, with fondness, people performing on the waste ground in the city centre, where they attracted large crowds who watched in wonderment. There were escapologists, acrobats, jugglers etc. and sometimes a one-man band. Also, there was a man who used to tear very thick telephone directories in half with his bare hands, and it was painful just watching him! After 14 years, food rationing ended on July 4th 1954 – nine years after the end of World War II.

Day Tripper

I attended Broadgreen Road Infants School, aka the "Tin School", in the Old Swan district of Liverpool. The daily three mile trip from Liverpool 8 meant that I had to get two trams to get there early each morning with my

The original Penny Lane roundabout

mother. The first tram (No. 5) took me to the Penny Lane roundabout, where I then changed over to the Old Swan tram, No 49. Of course, I didn't know that Penny

The No 5 tram which took me to Penny Lane roundabout

Lane would play a significant part of my life in the years ahead. After dropping me off at my Grandma's, my mum would make her way to work at the nearby Meccano factory at Binns Road.

The No 49 tram that took me to Old Swan

My Grandma always had a large pan of lovely porridge gently bubbling away on the gas oven, and I used to eat as much as possible before making my way from her house to school.

I Should Have Known Better

In later years, I attended Granby Street School where entertainers such as Lita Roza, Frankie Vaughan, Leonard Rossiter and others had been pupils. Liverpool, and in particular Liverpool 8, is renowned for its huge contribution to the world of entertainment, with its almost production-like line of comedians, actors and musicians hailing from this area. Lita Roza had the hit with a cover version of "How Much Is That Doggie In The Window" and I recall one summer day when she visited Granby Street School in a huge pink American limo. It seemed that all of the schoolchildren had come out to see the car, and Lita, of course.

Granby Street was a tough school in those days, with kids from a variety of backgrounds, and, like most schools, it had its share of school bullies. In fact, some of the teachers were bullies in their own right, and they loved nothing better than to deal out 'six of the best' for what, at the time seemed to be trivial offences. The canes that some of the teachers used were solid lengths of dowel, and they certainly left their mark.

I was relieved to pass what was then the 'thirteen plus' examination. It got me out of the "clutches" of Granby Street School's bullies and gained me entrance to the

Liverpool Junior School of Art at Gambier Terrace in Liverpool 8, opposite the Anglican Cathedral which was under construction: a much gentler environment altogether. Ironically, the day before I received the news that I had passed the entrance exam, the headmaster thrashed me again with his cane. I should have known better, because I had brought some American comics into school to swap, and he found out.

Everyone knew he hated American comics with their 'dreadful' slang and he always told us to read English comics, such as the *Eagle,* instead. Once inside his office, he started caning me, and if I pulled my hand away making him miss, he became more enraged and added extra strokes. By this time, he would be cursing and shouting, and obviously getting a big kick out of it all.

Gambier Terrace, where the Junior Art College was situated

At assembly the very next day, the headmaster proudly told all of the school what a wonderful pupil I was, being the first ever from Granby Street to pass the art exam and go to Art School.

There was no mention of the previous day's beating, and I felt like shouting; "No more aching fingers", but I thought better of it.

An atmospheric view of Gambier Terrace as John would have known it in the 60's

Gambier Terrace is a lovely Grade 2 listed Georgian terrace where, further along from our school, in the early '60s, John Lennon and Stuart Sutcliffe resided at number 3, Hillary Mansions, Gambier Terrace, while attending the senior Art College.

Bill Harry, who later created the *Mersey Beat* newspaper in 1961 was in the form above me at the Junior Art School in Gambier Terrace and we would sometimes meet and have a chat in the school yard, although he won't remember me after all these years.

I left Art School in 1954 when I was 15, because I was eager to start work and earn some money, so I took up screen-printing and poster writing.

No.3 Hillary Mansions, Gambier Terrace, where John Lennon and Stuart Sutcliffe lived

In my first job at a publicity studio, I was what is known as the 'can lad', which meant that I did all the fetching and carrying for the men, in between learning my trade.

Every Friday I would have to deliver advertising posters to many of the cinemas in and around Liverpool.

In front of the Art College are The Hope Street Suitcases created by John King and displayed there since 1998. Each case bears the name of a famous local person including the Fab Four, and they are a tourist attraction in their own right

Some were local, but lots were out of the city centre and I had to travel around by bus. It was always a slog because the rolls of posters could be quite heavy.

I used to get home late on Fridays, but I always used to get complimentary tickets at each cinema that I could share with my mates. For a year or so we all lived in the cinemas as often as time would allow until I changed my job, which meant that I lost the tickets as well as some of my so-called mates! Anyway, it wasn't too long before I met up with Colin Hanton and the rest of the Quarrymen. As one door shuts, another opens, as they say.

Another view of the Art College and the Magical Mystery coach

The Pier Head in 1952, opposite the Liver building is Tower Building, once the home of Kev Hanson, where we would spend many late nights listening to his records.

Photo of the Grade 1 listed Royal Liver Building today

The famous Royal Liver Building was opened on the 19th July 1911, and it has Grade 1 listed status.

There are two mythical Liver Birds, and it is said that one looks over the city to protect its people, the other looks out to sea keeping watch for incoming sailors.

Another story is that one is male, looking inland to see if the pubs are open, and the other is female looking out to sea for any handsome sailors coming into port.

By far, the most popular story is the one that claims if one of the birds were to fly away, the City of Liverpool would cease to exist.

ALL TOGETHER NOW
Meeting Colin

Colin Hanton, 1957

NOT TOO SURE when I first met Colin: it was some time in '56 through a mutual friend, Kevin Hanson. I was just an innocent teenager from Liverpool 8, until I met these two, but without them, my teenage years would have been uneventful. Kevin's dad was the caretaker at Tower Building, which is opposite the Royal Liver Building on the Strand.

They lived at the very top and when the Liver Building's clock chimed, everywhere seemed to vibrate. We used to go there late at night and Kev would play some of his large collection of LPs. Big Bill Broonzy was a favourite, as were the unusual records by real chain gangs.

In contrast, Colin lived in the leafy southern suburb of Woolton. When I used to visit him at his home, my bus ride would take me once again through the Penny Lane roundabout , as it did in my early school years, but this time, I would continue down to the leafy streets of Woolton.

Colin Hanton was in the group from the summer of '56 along with John Lennon, Eric Griffiths, Pete Shotton, Len Garry and Rod Davis.

Colin stayed with the group through several line-up changes until March 1959 (and by this time the band consisted of Colin, John Lennon, Paul McCartney, George Harrison and John Duff Lowe).

I would walk down Kings Drive towards his house and, as I neared, I could usually hear Colin through the open windows, practising on his drums. It was such a quiet area and I used to wonder what his tolerant neighbours must have thought, as Colin pounded away, unaware that he may be disturbing anybody.

Our main pubs were in the city centre and the ones nearest to the Cavern; usually the Grapes in Mathew Street on the opposite side and the White Star round the corner on Rainford Gardens. These two pubs in particular were always crammed to the doors, especially at weekends. Colin was the smaller of the three of us and, although he was the oldest, he looked younger. He was often asked his age in pubs, and so he took to carrying a copy of his birth certificate with him when we went out for a drink.

Once Colin got started on his favourite 'black velvets', he would usually drink us under the table, so to speak. Contrary to what has been claimed elsewhere, I never introduced Colin to black velvets. I had a small taste of the stuff once and it was awful, heavy and sickly, and it was so potent. I wouldn't recommend it to anyone. Colin, as honest as the day is long, still thinks that I introduced him to the demon drink. After such a long time, his memory has become a little clouded; not surprising, considering the amount of alcohol that we used to consume!

When we decided to stay in the suburbs, one of Woolton's oldest hotels/pubs is The Elephant on Woolton Street. It always looked a little austere to us and on the one occasion that I remember venturing inside with some of The Quarrymen, we were quickly shown the door. "Come back in a few years" one of the staff shouted, as we scuttled away toward the centre of the village. We quietly slipped into Woolton's oldest surviving pub, The Coffee House, which was always filled with cigarette smoke and resembled a foggy night. As usual, it was very busy and nobody seemed concerned that we were under age, so we all got our drinks and stood in the far corner of the room.

We had downed our first drink when someone said the police were in the Village, so we all vacated The Coffee House pretty quickly, although once outside, there was no sign of any police. The lads suggested that Pete Shotten had made it up, as it was his round next, but Pete denied all knowledge.

A No 5 bus that the Quarrymen would catch to travel home to Woolton Village

Sleepy Woolton Village around 1900 with the Woolton Hotel (now The Elephant) on the left. It would be just over 60 years later when John and the Quarrymen were to put Woolton on the international tourist map. The hotel is believed to date back to around 1770

There were many pubs in Woolton at the time, and some of them still survive; the Coffee House with the low ceilings was the smokiest of them all. Although some of us smoked, we used to cough when we went inside.

On one occasion in early 1957, Kev told us of party in Kingsley Road, Liverpool 8, which was close to my house and to which we were all invited. I don't know what the party was for, but in Liverpool, you don't need a reason to hold one and I went along with Kev, Colin and John Lennon. After a few drinks at the Clock pub on Kingsley Road, we made our way to the party, just along the road. It was cold and dark when we arrived and the house was overcrowded.

Kevin Hanson and me

The music was blaring out loud and it was very hot once inside. We hung our jackets on the hall-stand, only to find that there was no drink left. After a while, we made our way through the revellers to reach the record player. As we were looking through the assortment of records, a big guy asked in a loud voice, what we thought we were doing. He shouted that it was not our party, nor our place to organise the 'effing' records.

Before we had time to reply, he told us to get out, and by this time, a number of his mates had come over, so we didn't argue. In what seemed no time at all, we were bundled out onto the street.

It was cold outside and we realised that our jackets were still hanging up on the hall-stand inside the house, and we were only in our shirts. Colin asked; 'who's going to knock and ask for our jackets back'. Kev said; 'Charlie and John are the biggest', which was true, but we weren't brave enough to go on our own. There was a lot more of them and bigger too, and so we all went together trying to look hard. We knocked and waited but the loud music was drowning our efforts out.

Eventually, we banged on the door, trying to look even harder and more aggressive. John said: 'I wasn't ever going to come to Liverpool 8 again after the trouble at your street party Robbo' (that was my nickname at the time). When the door finally opened we were all expecting big trouble. 'Can we have our jackets back please?' we asked timidly, all thoughts of acting hard had long gone. To our great surprise, there was no real problem and our jackets were thrown out at us with the parting shout 'now sod off', which we did, very quickly, in case they changed their mind. It was then that John suggested we should have taken them all on, with a typical mischievous smirk.

We quickly made our way to Princes Avenue to the bus stop at the corner of Granby Street. Colin and John were anxious to catch a bus to the Penny Lane roundabout, where they could change to a number 5 that would take them home to the safety of Woolton.

When a bus arrived, they were relieved to get on it. Kev crossed over the avenue to catch his bus home to the Pier Head. I hurried along Granby Street to my home in Rosebery Street as quickly as I could.

A sunny day on Granby Street in the 1960s

YESTERDAY
The Skiffle Boom 1956-1958

I N TODAY'S MUSICAL world of synthesisers, computers and expensive amplifiers, back in the day, the idea of creating music in the mid 1950's with a washboard and tea chest seems laughable now: but it wasn't always so. Arguably, the most humble of music forms, 'skiffle' became a contemporary mainstay at this time, largely due to the success and exposure of the great Lonnie Donegan.

Because it was easy to play, and more importantly, cheap to start up a group, teenagers all over the country started practicing skiffle music, attempting to emulate Lonnie Donegan's style. Many of the groups eventually became famous in their own right.

Lonnie Donegan

Between 1956 and 1962, the 'King of Skiffle' had 26 hits, and it was during this time that John and the Quarrymen were into Elvis, Little Richard and the like. American rock 'n' roll and skiffle were now major influences for most of the new groups on the scene. By 1959, the skiffle bubble had burst. With its demise a new sound had emerged - 'Merseybeat' - and it was taking over the charts.

In November 1956, Lonnie Donegan was scheduled to appear at the Liverpool Empire. The advert in the *Liverpool Echo* at that time read; "Direct from his Terrific American Success": and two teenagers in particular were desperate for tickets. Both were big Donegan fans, and had already developed a taste for his music, but they had completely different motives for wanting to see him.

The 14-year-old Paul McCartney had recently lost his mother, and was looking for any means to escape his grief and sorrow, whereas 13-year-old George Harrison wanted inspiration, as he doubted his own skills of mastering his guitar, even at that early age.

Paul and George attended the same school, the Liverpool Institute High School (now LIPA) on Mount Street, and they met on the bus going to school. Their mutual love of Lonnie Donegan helped cement their friendship.

George's brother, Harry, and Harry's girlfriend, Irene McCann, were aware of George's obsession with guitars and his struggle to learn to play, so they bought him a ticket to the Lonnie Donegan show in the hope that it would encourage him to keep at it. During the show, George was mesmerised with Donegan, and studied what Lonnie was doing. Not just how he worked a crowd, but even down to memorising chord changes.

Paul was also lucky enough to acquire a ticket, and he came out of the show a new person. He had a focus that had been missing and the very next day, while sitting in his back garden thinking of his mum who had died a few days earlier at the young age of 47, he started strumming his guitar. It was said by Paul in later years, that was when he wrote his first song titled, "I Lost My Little Girl".

One teenager who wasn't fortunate enough to get a ticket for the show was 16 year old John Lennon. While he still revered Lonnie Donegan highly in his inspirations, John was, by this time, busy forming his own skiffle group with some of his school friends from Quarry Bank High School.

The newly formed group settled on the name The Quarrymen, which was the first line from the school song ,"The Song of the Quarry": "Quarrymen old before our birth, straining each muscle and sinew".

Along with The Quarrymen, lots of other Merseyside teenagers realised what was happening and they jumped at the chance of creating their own skiffle groups.

Richard Starkey, aka Ringo Starr, was working in a factory in the Dingle, Liverpool, and during his lunchtime, he played drums when a few friends would jam along with him. They were the Eddie Clayton Skiffle Group.

Such was the joy of skiffle, with its simplicity and honesty, it inspired so many teenagers, and is still considered an important genre in today's world.

The Quarrymen and the Eddie Clayton Skiffle Group weren't the only ones and within a short period of time, many others emerged across the city. They had some great names, such as; The Memphis City Group, The Dark Town Skiffle Group, Tommy "The Cherub" Smith and The Rockers, The Talismen, The Blue Genes Skiffle Group, The Raving Texans, The Deltic Skiffle Group and The Demons Skiffle Group to name but a few.

A number of these early skiffle groups evolved into the Merseybeat groups of the 1960's, and many became famous locally, while others achieved national and international fame.

The Raving Texans became Rory Storm and the Hurricanes who were more popular in Liverpool than The Beatles for a while, until both groups returned from their exploits in Hamburg when The Beatles became more popular than ever. The fans in Liverpool adored them and the Beatles were deemed to be much better musicians.

The Deltic Skiffle Group at Garston Baths, Liverpool

The Demons Skiffle Group from Childwall, Liverpool

Alan Caldwell, aka Rory Storm

Ringo joined the Beatles from the Hurricanes in August 1962 when he replaced Pete Best, after which The Beatles went on to worldwide fame and the Hurricanes were left in their wake. The Blue Genes Skiffle Group, after some slight name changes, eventually became the Swinging Blue Jeans and of course, The Quarrymen became The Beatles.

There were lots of venues in Liverpool to play, from garden fetes, clubs, pubs, parties and dance halls, and

Rory Storm and the Hurricanes, with Ringo on drums

many groups, including The Quarrymen, were so keen for success and recognition, they would appear for free on lots of occasions.

In November 2002, Lonnie, the man who inspired a generation to pick up their guitars, sadly passed away. What a legacy he created.

As George Harrison said:

**"Without Lonnie Donegan,
No Beatles"**

WITH A LITTLE HELP
The Practice Sessions

John being photographed by me

A MUTUAL FRIEND AND a big Quarrymen fan, Arthur Wong, was allowed by his parents to let The Quarrymen hold some practice sessions in the front room of their house in Mossley Hill. I went along with Colin, and Arthur was keen to show us his new Grundig reel-to-reel tape recorder. We were both amazed when Arthur gave us a demonstration, as this was state of the art recording equipment at the time, something that we could never have afforded. Colin set up his drum kit and eventually the rest of the lads arrived together; John, Len, Eric, Pete and Rod.

Everyone juggled the seats around to accommodate the gear, and there wasn't much room left, especially when Len brought his tea chest in. They all knew Arthur Wong, but they didn't know me.

"Alright Charlie, what do you play?" "I can't play anything", I replied. "Neither can this lot, so you'll be alright."

John Lennon

"This is a mate of mine, Charlie Roberts", said Colin. John said "alright Charlie, what do you play?"

"I can't play anything", I replied. "Neither can this lot, so you'll be alright," said John, and it broke the ice. Everyone fell about laughing, including me.

Very soon, I was to learn that such off the cuff quips like this were typical of John, and his witty sarcasm was often the source of the bands failure to take future rehearsals seriously.

To be honest, John's remark wasn't far from the truth, as the lads were only beginners, which was the reason for their practice sessions after all. Pete knew how to wind John up on occasions, and I remember him repeatedly telling one of his stock jokes to John; "she was only the Eskimos daughter" he would shout, and John would quickly reply; "but she had an icicle bum".

"How did you know that?" Pete would ask, with a typical smirk on his face. "Because you have told me enough times already," John would shout, looking quite annoyed. Pete would sooner or later repeat the joke and get a similar reaction from John on each occasion. Most of the practice sessions that I attended were like that, with lots of larking around, although when they were being serious, Arthur, ever protective of his new recorder, would switch the Grundig on and tape them.

We would listen to the tapes with Arthur during the next day or so, then Arthur would erase them, ready for the next session. Nobody would have wanted them, recordings by six young unknown lads, singing and larking about in 1957, would they?

One evening during practice, Arthur left the room and John was curious to see how this new-fangled tape actually worked. The lads had never used one before, and John was on his knees, fiddling around with the controls: "It's not workin'," he said. The lads started winding him up saying that he must have broken it. "I hardly touched it," said John in a bit of a panic. "You've had it now! Wait until Arthur comes back in," we said jokingly, but John was by now getting worried that he had done some damage to the recorder.

John then tried to encourage everyone to pack up and leave, before Arthur returned. As they started to collect their gear, Arthur came back in and asked; "What's up? Where are you all going?" "We think the recorder is broken; it won't play," someone said. John was looking sheepish; "I didn't do anything, honest," he said, and for a moment, everything went very quiet. "Don't say that, me dad will go mad! I only just got it," raged Arthur, with a mischievous look on his face. He calmly reached behind the settee and said; "you need to turn the power on, soft lad". Arthur had switched it off before leaving the room. I never again saw John as relieved as he was that day, and now everyone was buzzing and acting the fool once again – normality had returned!

Most of the early sessions consisted of about 10% serious practice and 90% larking around. In time, they would become more serious and professional, but for now they were just a group of lads having fun with no pretensions of being taken seriously. I remember that Colin would become quite annoyed (and who could blame him) because, after making the effort to carry his drum kit on and off the bus, he would arrive at the practice venue only to find everyone fooling around.

Hardly any real practice would take place and the wasted journey was then repeated in reverse. Colin used to wonder if it was worth all the effort, but, thankfully, he persevered. Of course, Colin's favourite practice sessions were at his own house on Saturdays when his mum was out shopping and he didn't have to carry his drums on the buses.

I used to work at Littlewoods in Crosby as a printer and at that time, my boss was Arthur Davis (Mr. Davis to me) who was great on the piano with his boogie woogie/rock 'n roll style. I used to tell him about The Quarrymen, and he became quite interested, so much so that he asked if he could attend a practice session.

In the beginning, everyone was welcome and so Arthur Davis came to two sessions at Arthur Wong's house. He played a few numbers on the piano and everyone seemed to like it, although, as usual, nothing was taken seriously. Arthur tried again at the next session and attempted to get the lads to settle down and play a few numbers in unison, at least. His efforts were in vain and he decided not to bother again because he saw no future in it. Understandably, nobody could have possibly foreseen what the future held for John and his Quarrymen. When The Beatles became the biggest band in history, Mr. Davis once asked me; "Is that John who started with those Quarrymen, the ones who were always messing around?" When I confirmed it, he looked a little deflated. I seem to remember that John was not keen to have a piano in the group.

A month or so later, after I had just finished my tea, there was a knock on the front door at Rosebery Street. It was Arthur Wong with a huge beaming smile on his face. "Alright Charlie, what d'you think?" he said, and I poked my head out of the doorway to see a brand new car. "Whose is that?" I asked. "Mine," said Arthur, "dad bought it for me for my 17th birthday".

A Vauxhall Cresta, similar to Arthur's birthday present

This wasn't just any car: it was a flashy, two-tone Vauxhall Cresta with white wall tyres and rear fins – the nearest thing to an American car that any of us had ever seen.

I was disappointed when Arthur didn't take me for a spin, but he had to get home before his dad returned. "Dad's going away on business tomorrow for a few days, so I will pick you up on Friday night, and we'll shoot down to Lennon's," said Arthur.

By the time Arthur got back into his car it was surrounded by lots of kids who had never seen the like before. It may seem hard to believe, but in 1957 there was only one old private car in the whole of Rosebery Street. Little wonder that Arthur's Cresta was the focus of so much attention.

In the meantime, Rosebery Street was about to be transformed for a street party we would never forget.

RUN FOR YOUR LIFE
Rosebery Street - 22nd June 1957

Me outside my house at 84, Rosebery Street, with the very first publicity poster advertising the Quarrymen Skiffle Group's performance in our street

OUR STREET PARTY was held to celebrate the 750th anniversary of King John issuing Liverpool with a Royal Charter, to give Liverpool status as a borough; Liverpool was born in 1207. Since my mum was the head of our street's committee, I had asked The Quarrymen if they would play at the street party.

Although they were a bit hesitant because the area of Liverpool 8 had a bad reputation, I persuaded them that they would be safe. It should be remembered at this point that some of the lads were still at school and were not streetwise or accustomed to violence. To their credit, they agreed to the 'booking', and arranged some practice sessions a week or so before.

The promotional poster that I hand-wrote for the occasion and which sat in our front window at number 84 generated a lot of interest. The poster was effective because at the time not many people knew much about

STREET PARTY
COMM 4 PM SAT. JUNE 22

RACES *
RECORDS * SONGS
FANCY DRESS * LUCKY DIP
DANCING * PRIZES
GAMES ETC.

SPECIAL ATTRACTION 5 PM

QUARRYMEN
Skiffle Group!

Recreation of Charlie's poster

skiffle music, and nobody in the area had ever seen a live skiffle group. Nor had anyone in the area heard of the Quarrymen before, and of course, neither had most of Liverpool.

Neighbours asked me; "Who are the Quarrymen and what do they do?" To which I would proudly answer, "they are a skiffle group and they're my mates".

Most of them were none the wiser! Little did they, or anyone else for that matter, know that they were about to witness a performance by the group that would eventually evolve into the greatest band in the world – ever!

During the week before the party, my family and most of our neighbours were busy decorating the street in readiness for the big day ahead. My mum collected a weekly amount of money from the neighbours which was used to buy the food and drinks.

The big day finally arrived and the sun shone brightly and everyone was excited in anticipation of what was to come later. A band coming to play in our little street: who would have believed it?

Neighbours and their families were all busy with the

final preparations and the excitement was mounting. Many street parties had been held in Rosebery Street in the past, but they were never as grand as this one.

About 12 noon, the tables were set, the food and drink was brought out and everyone started to take their seats.

Although food rationing ended in 1954, 9 years since the end of the 2nd World War, certain foods were still hard to come by, especially in the poorer areas of Liverpool. But today was different, with a large variety of mouth-watering goodies laid out across the tables.

My mum had organised a weekly collection, which was used to buy the more expensive food, not normally affordable in Liverpool 8. There was plenty to eat (for once), unlike most days when, if you didn't like what was served up, there was no second choice, and that would be it until the next day. How times have changed.

There were the usual party games with prizes to be won and the youngsters were all eager to get involved, but the older element were waiting for the skiffle group to arrive.

It was around 3.15pm when, to their credit, The Quarrymen sheepishly turned into Rosebery Street, having just visited the Windsor Hotel aka 'The Clock' pub on Kingsley Road, where they 'had a few' for a bit of Dutch courage. I could tell that they had been drinking, as I ushered them into my house at number 84, where my mum, Marjorie Roberts, plied the lads

The Windsor Hotel, also known as "The Clock", on Kingsley Road in Liverpool 8, close to Rosebery Street, where The Quarrymen went for a drink before their performance

My mother at the top of the ladder, with Charlie passing up the photograph

with food and drink (tea or coffee that is) and definitely no more alcohol. We were all in a jovial mood, and although rather apprehensive, the lads were eager to get started.

Colin knew the area, as he had visited and stayed at mine before, so he wasn't as nervous as the others. This was, after all, the first ever outdoor booking for The Quarrymen: John claimed in *Anthology* that it was their very first appearance , although they had, in fact, played at some other venues previously, like The Cavern Club and the Liverpool Empire.

Once the Quarrymen had finished off the food, they spent a while tuning up amid laughing, joking and general fooling around. They had used up a lot of time during the previous week practicing for their

Some of the locals in the now decorated Rosebery Street on 22nd June 1957, preparing for the party.

appearance at what was to become a truly historic event in the story of The Beatles. Claims that, after a suggestion by John, they were calling themselves 'Johnny and the Rainbows' on this occasion are untrue. They were the Quarrymen and their name can be seen quite clearly printed on Colin's drum in the photograph of the event.

As a matter of fact, I was the one who had painted that name lettering onto Colin's bass drumhead.

Time was up, and the six lads filed out of number 84 and went left down to number 76 and the flatback wagon. The wagon belonged to Mr. Fred Tyrer, who had also provided the basic microphone that was powered from a music system in his front room. The wagon itself was not as dirty as had been suggested in some previous

John Lennon and The Quarrymen in Rosebery Street 1957

publications. It wasn't a coal wagon, but was normally used to transport all manner of goods, but never coal! It was beginning to get noisy while the Quarrymen were setting up, with lots of excited kids waiting in anticipation. At this point, Pete said that they weren't due to start until 5pm and it was only 4.00pm. John replied; "It makes a change for us, we're usually late".

Colin was practising what he used to tell me were 'rim shots' while Len was preparing to support John with some vocals.

As a large crowd was now gathering and after a brief discussion, it was decided that they should get started. John Lennon, in his customary check shirt took centre stage with his guitar. Colin Hanton on drums and Len Garry on tea chest bass, who were both sporting crew cuts, were at the side and the rear respectively.

The remaining Quarrymen - Eric Griffiths on guitar, Rod Davis on banjo, and Pete Shotton on washboard - surrounded John near the front of the crowded flat-back wagon. John, of course, was on the microphone at the front. The audience were in awe as the lads started playing a mixture of mostly skiffle and a little rock 'n' roll. They kicked off with the "Midnight Special" as it was one of their favourites, followed by other popular skiffle songs of the day, "Railroad Bill", "Maggie May", an old Liverpool shanty, "Freight Train" and the like.

At the time, for most of the latest songs, it was difficult to know the correct words and the only way to learn them was to listen to them repeatedly on the radio or

A Kodak Brownie camera like t[he] one I used

gramophone. As a result, John would quite often make up the words of the songs as he went along when he didn't know the correct ones. Most of the audience never knew anything different, and so he always got away with it.

After about 45 minutes of music and joking around, the lads took a well earned rest.

During the break, the local girls chatted and flirted with the Quarrymen and the lads liked all of the attention. John and Pete were obviously loving it; Len and Colin were not that far behind. Rod and Eric were a little more reserved and they really only wanted to get started on the second half performance.

The lads finally assembled on the wagon for the second time and off they went again. Back then, there was little noise from traffic, and so the Quarrymen could easily be heard in the nearby streets. The music quickly attracted crowds from these streets including a tough gang of black lads from neighbouring Hatherley Street.

Living in the next street, I had encountered them many times before, as many of them went to Granby Street School with me, so I was not concerned at that stage.

The Rosebery Street lads were always nervous when they were around though, but our skirmishes with them never amounted to much, just a bit of name-calling and stone throwing. They hardly ever came into our street and we never went into theirs!

Although we were "territorial enemies", we all used to get on well at school in Granby Street, with no hint of trouble between any of us.

After a few numbers, Colin sensed that something was wrong. He shouted to some lads and asked 'what was going on'- they shouted back 'they're going to get Lennon'.

John stares at the camera as Charlie takes the photo

Until then, the atmosphere was great, even though there was a lot of pushing and shoving as the audience tried to get nearer to the 'stage'. The Quarrymen appeared to be really enjoying themselves, with John and Pete giving it loads, playing to their over enthusiastic audience. Nearing the end of the second half it seemed as if 'that Lennon' had been winking at the girls in the audience, but John always emphatically denied this claim. John being short sighted, may have just been squinting, as was often the case, and for once, I believed him.

Whatever the cause, and with the tension quickly building with the lads in the crowd, the terrified Quarrymen finished their final number and quickly jumped off the wagon and ran for their lives to take cover back in my house at number 84. The crowd wanted more, but the Quarrymen didn't!

The lads were visibly shaken and so the set after tea was quickly abandoned, This had been their first experience of threatened violence, but it wasn't to be their last.
The Quarrymen weren't at all street wise unlike the gang that was after them, and they were so grateful to be able to take shelter in my house. "I thought you said we'd be alright Charlie" said Pete. "You wouldn't have turned up if I had told you any different," I replied.

Meanwhile, Mr. Tyrer had uncoupled the microphone and driven the wagon around the block to where the remaining equipment was brought up the jigger (Scouse for back entry) and into the rear of 84.

More food and drink was served and later, with no sign of the gang moving from outside, someone suggested that we should all go out to the front and face up to the gang. "Count me out" said Pete, and the rest of us hastily agreed. The police, nicknamed "Scuffers" in Liverpool, were eventually called and a lone policeman arrived to escort the Quarrymen (minus Colin) up Rosebery Street to their bus stop on Princes Avenue, where they caught their bus back home to the safety of Woolton.

Back then, and unlike today, the sight of even one policeman was enough to deter violent gangs. Colin had gone missing and it turned out that he had copped off with a girl, Norma Hanson (no relation to our mate Kevin), from further down the street. I don't remember where he left his drum kit, but Colin told me he packed it up and took it to Norma's house during all the confusion.

From all accounts there was a good old fashioned knees-up with the Hanson family into the early hours of Sunday morning. The Hansons were always game for a few drinks and a sing-a-long without any reason.

Most reports claim that the Quarrymen were not invited back for the following weekend when the Council funded another party at Rosebery Street, as it was voted the best decorated street in Liverpool. This claim was untrue, as the Quarrymen were invited back by me, but after their first experience, they didn't fancy a return visit: ONCE WAS ENOUGH! And anyway, Colin had forgotten about the band, as he had met his new love-Norma!

On the following Saturday and in place of the Quarrymen, the great Merseysippi Jazz Band were excellent substitutes. There are many published accounts about this day and some are highly dubious. Claims that some of the audience were dancing on the flat back truck are untrue. With six Quarrymen and their gear, guitars, drum kit and tea chest there was barely enough room for them, let alone people dancing! It has also been claimed that the Quarrymen were all 'effing and blinding' during and after their performance. At that stage in their lives, the Quarrymen, including John, did not swear in public and I certainly never heard any of them use the 'F' word, as has been claimed by some authors eager to sensationalise their latest book.

Claims that Paul was at the Rosebery Street Party are wrong. In the photograph on page 55, there is a lad in the bottom right hand corner who bears a resemblance to Paul McCartney, but it was NOT Paul. Paul would not have dared to venture into Liverpool 8 on his own and never once mentioned having seen the Quarrymen there. He didn't meet John until two weeks later when they first met at St. Peters on 6th July 1957.

Over the decades, many simple stories have evolved into exaggerated tales made up by would-be Beatle authors who have no first hand knowledge to back up their claims, just their "research" - or should I say plagiarism? The trouble is, once such false claims are in print, sadly, most fans believe them to be the truth!

The day after the party, I was stopped by some of the lads from neighbouring Hatherley Street. "Hey Robbo, come 'ere" they shouted, and I didn't dare disobey. They wanted to know where that Lennon feller lived. I told them that I only knew him from the Cavern, and thankfully they believed me. They told me that if I did see him again to warn him that if he ever set foot in Liverpool 8 again, they would break his 'effing legs.

When I told John about the confrontation, he went a bit pale and then said that he wouldn't go near Liverpool 8 ever again! History shows that he did return on a

The third of my photographs of The Quarrymen

number of occasions, performing at the wonderful Rialto Ballroom and other venues in and around Liverpool 8. He attended a house party in Kingsley Road as well as a party at my house, the scene of the original 'siege'. John also lived at Gambier Terrace on the fringe of Liverpool 8 when he was at Art School. Fortunately, he never crossed paths with the Hatherley Street crew again.

The Rialto Theatre and Ballroom was opened in 1927 and eventually closed in late 1964. As rock 'n' roll music gained popularity in early 1956, the Rialto started Sunday afternoon sessions which attracted youths from all parts of Merseyside, eager to dance to the latest American hit records. After it's closure, the Rialto was converted into an antique furniture showroom until the final curtain in 1981. During the Toxteth riots that summer, the Rialto was burnt down by arsonists. The

The Rialto Cinema and Ballroom

theatre could seat over 1800 and the ballroom could accommodate 500 dancers.

Like so many venues that The Quarrymen/Beatles played on Merseyside, it was sadly gone forever. All we have left are the memories of clubs, pubs and other venues that are nearly all gone or converted. A couple of hundred yards away from the Rialto, along Princes Avenue, was Rosebery Street, long since demolished except for a couple of houses on each side at the top end, on the avenue. The street sign is still there, as is the bus stop.

It would only be two weeks after the Rosebery Street Party that, on the 6th of July, John would meet Paul McCartney at St. Peters Church at the annual 'Woolton Parish Church Garden Fete'.

The corner of Rosebery Street with Princes Avenue. The bus stop where the lads would catch their bus back to Woolton

COME GO WITH ME
The Day John Met Paul

Saturday 6th July 1957: St. Peter's Garden Fete

Poster from the Fete for 6th July 1957

THE GARDEN FETE at St. Peter's was a great day out with hot sunny weather. There were lots of people milling around Church Road and in the village as the wagons crawled very slowly around the streets.

The Rose Queen's wagon led the way followed by the Quarrymen playing their skiffle music. The wagons

Two photographs showing the Quarrymen heading along Kings Drive on the day of the fete. Top picture left to right-Pete Shotton, Eric Griffiths, Len Garry, John Lennon, Colin Hanton and Rod Davis. Bottom picture- John hasn't gone looking for a pub, he is hiding behind Len. Photographs courtesy Rod Davis.

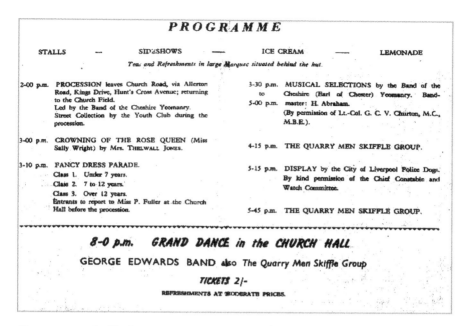

The programme for The Quarrymen's appearances on 6th July 1957

came back up Church Road then turned left and continued up the path that led to the field, where all the fun of the fete was to be found. Stalls, sideshows, candy floss, coconut shy, police dogs, games, fancy dress, military band and much more.

"Ivan Vaughan mentioned he was going to Woolton Parish Church to see this group he sometimes played with, though he wasn't actually playing. I said 'yes', I would come along." Paul McCartney.

During the afternoon, and in sharp contrast to the skiffle music, was the Band of the Cheshire Yeomanry, followed by the Quarrymen, who played their repertoire of about a dozen or so Skiffle numbers such as "Cumberland Gap,"

Ivan Vaughan was a childhood friend of John Lennon. He lived in Vale Road, directly behind John, who was in Menlove Avenue. He also attended Dovedale Primary School with John. Ivan moved on to The Liverpool Institute Grammar School, while John went to Quarry Bank School. It was at the Institute where he met and became friends with Paul McCartney and Len Garry. Ivan would often play tea chest bass with John and The Quarrymen, until Len took over as the bass player full time.

"Maggie May", "Railroad Bill", "Lost John" etc. They ended their set with a couple of rock 'n' roll hits that included "Be-Bop-a-Lula", according to a mutual friend of the Quarrymen, Ivan Vaughan. Ivan, who attended the Liverpool Institute Grammar School with Len Garry and Paul McCartney, invited Paul along to the fete with the intention of introducing him to his mate John Lennon, because of their shared interest in music.

What took place at the fete that day, as it pertains to John and Paul meeting, has been well documented, but often wrongly, and the truth is that nobody was aware that such a momentous occasion was about to take place later in the day.

Following their afternoon set, The Quarrymen had moved from the main field to set up in the church hall across the road from the church. Although Paul did meet John there, it was not for the first time that day. Colin remembers that John, Paul and Ivan talked briefly in the scout hut, before the much more famous 'meeting'. Most of the published accounts of the day and the meeting of John and Paul are from authors who weren't there, and many of whom were not even born at the time it took place!

Although we were all there, to put an exact time down, or quote what was said would be extremely difficult and almost impossible, as most of us don't remember much about it at all. Who could, after so long? After all, Paul was just another interested lad who meant nothing to us at the time, and so Paul turning up at St. Peter's was insignificant.

The lads were tuning up and the hall was being prepared for the evening dance, so it was quite noisy and most of us were totally unaware, or had little interest in what turned out to be the famous historic 'meeting'. However, I do remember some of the significant events that day.

A rare photo of the Quarrymen on stage for the afternoon set. In a couple of hours or so, John would meet Paul. "That was the day, the day that I met Paul that it started moving." JOHN LENNON

A lot of reports claim that Colin Hanton was not at the evening session, but they are entirely untrue. I was with the Quarrymen during the night, and Colin was definitely there; I could see him and hear him! Colin knows that his non-attendance was wrongly reported in a local newspaper at the time and I have to agree with his explanation.

The stage in St. Peter's Church Hall, where John met Paul

As always, he was positioned at the rear of the stage and the reporter, who was probably inexperienced, did not see him. Colin is not that big and, who knows, the reporter may have been smaller still and unable to see everything through the crowd.

Subsequent writers have latched on to the story and have included it in their books and articles.

Whatever happened to proper research?

All any author had to do was contact Colin for the truth about the most important event in Beatle history. I suppose it is easier to lift stories from other publications, whether true or false! The well-known cliché that "there would have been no Beatles without the Quarrymen" fails to recognise the fact that, but for Ivan Vaughan, a mutual friend of John and Paul who had the foresight to introduce Paul to John, the Quarrymen

Ivan (left) with Pete Shotton

as a group may well have folded.

There certainly would have been no Beatles as we now know them but for Ivan. From the time that Paul became involved, there was a renewed energy, more confidence and enthusiasm from the lads, even though bookings and gigs had dried up. John and Paul were on the same wavelength when it came to rock 'n' roll from the off.

They were very raw, but a partnership that was bound to flourish and grow into the greatest ever band on the planet.

Ivan Vaughan sadly died in 1993 from Parkinson's Disease.

However, for bringing Paul McCartney to meet John Lennon that day, we owe Ivan a huge debt of gratitude.

There are many stories associated with St. Peter's and Thelma Grant has been looking into them. She shared her findings with me.

Who Was Eleanor Rigby?

The Eleanor Rigby grave in St. Peter's churchyard, Church Road, Woolton, is one of the most visited graves in the kingdom. On average, 100 people visit every day. Why? The Beatles brought the name to fame. It was the inspiration for their famous song - wasn't it?

My friend Dave Peters, now sadly deceased, was a contemporary of John Lennon. Dave told me that he asked John if the song "Eleanor Rigby" was named from the gravestone. John said no, it was called after Eleanor Bron, the actress who made the film Help! with our four lads. Dave persisted; "but you spent a lot of time in the churchyard before you went in for choir practice. You must have noticed the gravestone with Eleanor Rigby on it. Think of the rhythm of the name. Eleanor Bron doesn't fit." John dragged on his cigarette. "Yeah, maybe you're right."

Paul McCartney also said the song was named after Eleanor Bron and Rigby was from Rigby and Evans Ltd., wine and spirit shippers of Bristol. But he did say he and John spent a lot of time in St. Peter's churchyard smoking and sunbathing.

So, who was the real Eleanor Rigby? Eleanor was born on 29th August 1895 and lived all her life in Woolton Village. She was up at 5am each workday morning and walked with a group of her friends to the original Royal Infirmary in town where she was employed as a scullery maid. Eleanor was not one of the lonely people. She married Thomas Woods in 1930. She sadly died, aged 44, on 10th October 1939 from a brain haemorrhage.

One of the houses Eleanor lived in is fourth up Vale Road from the Derby Arms pub. It was originally number 8. Due to re-numbering, when new properties were built, it is now number 225 Vale Road. It has a plain wooden door with the windows blanked out by white curtains.

The Choir

Paul failed his audition to sing in Liverpool Cathedral Choir. David Moore, one time organist in St. Peter's, passed! They sang scales and "Once in Royal David's City". There is a picture in the church hall of the two little boys.

Another dear friend of mine, Stella Hitchen, knew Mimi Smith, John's aunt. Stella told me that Mimi, a regular church member, encouraged John to take part in the choir and he did sing at some events - although he was thrown out for misbehaving. He used to hang around the churchyard smoking before sneaking quietly into church ducking down as he crept up the aisle and into his place at the far left of the choir stalls.

TWO OF US
Meeting Paul McCartney

Paul McCartney with The Quarrymen at Wilson Hall

IT MUST HAVE been around early August '57 when Arthur picked me up as arranged on the Friday evening.

I am certain that the date was early August because Paul McCartney had recently agreed to join the The Quarrymen. I carefully got into Arthur's car in case I did any damage. Once inside, there was an overpowering aroma of new wood and leather and the seats were very plush. To someone like me who was only used to riding on rickety old trams and buses, Arthur's Cresta was like a magic carpet. We set off for Menlove Avenue and during the journey (about 5 miles) we (the car, that is) received lots of admiring glances. We went along Granby Street, then Smithdown Road and on toward Penny Lane, before eventually turning into Menlove Avenue.

"George Harrison had a great haircut, he had this long hair that he quiffed back. We had a friend, Arthur, he used to describe it as a f""kin turban!, and it did, it looked like a big marvellous thing!" Paul McCartney.

It was a lovely, warm, sunny evening and as we neared Mendips, we could see Colin and John at the gate with the latest member of the Quarrymen: Paul McCartney.

All three took some time admiring the new car, and they were clearly impressed. They each took great care getting into the rear of the car, and everyone was in a happy mood as we cruised along Menlove Avenue, then into and around Woolton Village.

Arthur drove us around the village a few times and everyone we passed would stop and stare in amazement. The Cresta was beautiful and unique, even in "posh" Woolton, and was a real head turner. Nobody was interested in the passengers, a group of unknown teenagers posing and having a laugh; they just wanted to admire the car!

Paul had his guitar with him and throughout the journey he was practising a great Bill Justis instrumental called "Raunchy".

That song was, coincidentally, the same number played by George Harrison when he auditioned for the group.

I was quoted by one ill-informed author as having threatened Paul "that if he didn't stop playing 'Raunchy', I would throw him out of the car". What a load of rubbish, written by an author who had never even spoken to me. In fact, we encouraged Paul to continue because we enjoyed it, and he was practising to be able to play the instrumental at the next gig.

We had a number of similar trips during the next couple of weeks and Arthur was always concerned about us looking after his beautiful motor car. We did take care; we loved it nearly as much as Arthur did.

However….one evening, we pulled up outside Jo's Milk Bar in the village centre and we all got out. Somebody closed a rear door in the normal manner when the window shattered and the glass went everywhere. No one owned up, but it didn't really matter: it was an accident. There was glass inside the car, outside on the pavement and even inside the door panel.

Someone brought a brush and shovel from the milk bar and we hastily set about clearing up what we could. We couldn't do much about the inside of the car, as we didn't have a vacuum. Poor Arthur had turned pale with shock, worried about how his father would react. We tried to calm Arthur down, telling him that the glass must have been faulty and that it was an accident that could have happened to any one of us.

"Dad will murder me," said Arthur, becoming more distraught. The Grundig was a joke, but this is serious;

he won't believe it was an accident," he said. At this point we all nervously discussed what we could do to help, but we had to admit, we couldn't do anything. We attempted to reassure Arthur that his dad would understand, but he knew different.

Looking very worried, Arthur said he would have to go home to face the music and he dropped me off at Penny Lane on the way. "See you at John's tomorrow, if I'm still in one piece and the car is fixed," said Arthur, before he drove off home. All that he could do was to go home and tell the truth, which he did, but Mr. Wong would have none of it, believing that we had been clowning around. Arthur was grounded and we never got to ride the magic carpet again.

The public footpath steps leading up to the path across the quarry from Quarry Street

We didn't know until later, after waiting outside Mendips with John for what seemed a long time, that Arthur wasn't coming: so maybe the car was still out of action?

Arthur was, in fact, told he could not use the car to ferry his pals around anymore; it was strictly for him

1950's view of Woolton from the Quarry Street footpath

View of Woolton from Quarry Street footpath in 2017

and his family, which was understandable given the circumstances.

"Let's walk to Colin's," suggested John, "he'll be thinking we've forgotten about him."

We left John's and turned into nearby Vale Road where John said we should go up Castle Street to see his favourite view of Woolton. At the top of Castle Street, we crossed over Quarry Street to a public footpath that went over the quarry. I had never noticed it before, and to this day it is often overlooked. John said it was a short-cut to the village, although it would probably have been the same distance had we gone down Quarry Street and turned left at the bottom into the village.

When we reached the middle section of the footpath, which had high walls on either side, John stopped, and

2017: Woolton Quarry, now a housing estate, a far cry from the times when we would climb to the top, just for the view over Woolton

An early view of the Woolton Hotel, now The Elephant

1950's Woolton Quarry, in the background is St. Peters Church

Woolton Baths, Allerton Road, believed to be around 1900

1957:Woolton Village

standing on tip toes he looked over the wall and surveyed the view of Woolton.

"What do you think Charlie, it's great isn't it," said John, and I had to agree. "It's one of my favourite places, Woolton, the home of the Quarrymen. Not many people come up here and I can stay as long as I want. Sometimes, there is a brick or something to stand on, but we are tall enough anyway," said John.

"Pete doesn't like coming up here, but Shotton's a lazy sod, and it's a bit too much of a climb for him," John chuckled. I wondered just how much John could really see across the village, as he appeared to be squinting, as if he was trying to focus properly. We stayed a while, although it was quite humid and large black clouds were quickly gathering in the distance.

With this in mind, we decided not to go to Colin's and instead John hurried back to Mendips, while I caught the bus home from the Village. The public footpath is still there and is sign-posted, but it can easily be missed. Over the years, high wire mesh has been erected on either side of the footpath which is now covered with a variety of weeds and vegetation.

As a result it has become increasingly difficult to enjoy the view, and if you do visit, take something to stand on. If you wish to re-trace John's walk over the quarry, you can start at the Quarry Street end. The footpath will take you to New Mill Stile, which leads to Church Road. Turn right and a short walk downhill brings you to St.

Peter's Church, where Eleanor Rigby lies buried in the graveyard. On the opposite side is the church hall where John reportedly met Paul for the first time.

At the bottom of Church Road is the historic village of Woolton, where John and The Quarrymen naturally spent a lot of their time. One of their favourite places was the wonderful Woolton Picture House where John in particular spent a lot of time.

The cinema is still there, showing the latest films all these years later. I never witnessed it, but the story goes that John enjoyed the challenge of 'bunking in': something most young lads would try, if given half a chance.

The young Quarrymen loved to spend time at Woolton Picture House

Rock 'n' Roll Music

Statue of Elvis in Memphis

WHEN JOHN SAID the first gig that the Quarrymen played was at Rosebery Street, he was obviously mistaken. After so long, the memory can become confused and it is most likely that the first ever photos of the Quarrymen playing at the party had stuck in his memory, making him believe that it was their first ever performance.

There were, in fact, a number of performances before the 22nd June 1957 and I attended some of them. I cannot be certain about the exact dates, but I went to a Holyoake Hall show and also at St. Barnabas Church Hall before Rosebery Street. I did not attend when the lads appeared at the Liverpool Empire Theatre for the *Carroll Levis Discovery Show* or at the Cavern Club on occasions, but I am assured by those who were there that those were also before the street party.

In my teens, when I still lived in Rosebery Street, a guy used to call selling the latest records "cheaply", so I would buy whatever I could afford at the time. Where he got them from I didn't ask. He always had Elvis, Fats Domino, Little Richard, Buddy Holly, Jerry Lee Lewis and Chuck Berry and the like, who all had hits from the mid to late '50s onwards, and along with Lonnie Donegan they were hugely influential with the Quarrymen.

Elvis had a large string of hits beginning in 1956 including "Heartbreak Hotel", and when John Lennon first heard it he couldn't believe his ears. From that moment on he was in awe of almost everything Elvis recorded, and the dozens of hits continued to 1960,

giving John plenty of inspiration. At this time, John, like many other young teenage lads, wanted to be Elvis! And who could blame them? Elvis had the looks, the voice, the charisma and the girls that worshipped him.

I would lend John his favourite songs from my record collection, so that he could learn the words. Some of them I never got back from John, but I did not mind too much. I considered it to be fair exchange as I never had to pay whenever I went with the lads to their gigs, and he had probably worn them out anyway!

I'd been invited to see them play several times by Paul but for some reason, never got round to it before. I remember being very impressed with John's big thick sideburns and trendy teddy boy clothes. In a way, all that emotional rough stuff was simply a way for him to help separate the men from the boys, I think. I was never intimidated by him. Whenever he had a go at me, I just gave him a little bit of his own right back".
George Harrison

The American rock 'n' rollers from 1956 through to the early '60s were highly influential with John and Paul in particular. There had never been anything like it before. Bill Haley had many hits from 1954 through to '57, but Elvis, Little Richard, Jerry Lee Lewis, Chuck Berry, Buddy Holly and a host of others, now took rock 'n' roll to a new level, and some! John and the Quarrymen couldn't get enough of it.

Another source of American records at the

time was from black USAAF airmen who were based at RAF Burtonwood in Warrington close to Liverpool. There were up to 1,800 American airmen based at Burtonwood after the Second World War, and some lived in and around Mulgrave Street in Liverpool 8.

I often used to get American comics from them and sometimes the latest record or two. When we couldn't get the latest records, we would listen to a commercial station, Radio Luxembourg, but reception was always quite poor and continually fading in and out. Sometimes it would mean listening for the same record to be played again later that day or even the next day, to write all of the words down correctly. It was very time-consuming and not always possible, which is why John used to make the words up on occasions. From the late '50s into the early '60s, from The Quarrymen then onto The Beatles, the lads must have appeared at almost every club on Merseyside.

They also played at numerous events, such as house parties and weddings. Sadly, most of the places have long since gone; some demolished, others turned into shops, and some even supermarkets. Many of the club appearances were never fully advertised: the posters would just say something like "Skiffle Night" with 4 groups, and then the name of the artists would not be mentioned. Little or no documentation exists, so it is difficult and mostly impossible to say when and where they played on such occasions. A lot is down to memory, and sometimes even that can be distorted, with many claims being misleading hearsay.

What is correctly reported is that George Harrison was a school friend of Paul McCartney from the Liverpool Institute Grammar School. George was born on 25th February, 1943, so was less than a year younger than Paul, and two and a half years younger than John. George joined The Quarrymen at the end of 1957. George would always be around their gigs and he was often at Wilson Hall, Garston, with his guitar, just watching the groups: he was soon, after an audition on the top deck of a bus, a member of The Quarrymen.

WILSON HALL – Speke Road, Garston.

THE TOUGHEST VENUE THAT THE QUARRYMEN PLAYED?

Soon after Paul McCartney joined The Quarrymen, his influence was beginning to show. They were becoming more professional in the way they dressed as well as their on-stage presence. Paul, being left-handed, stood to the right of John who was right-handed. They both had a microphone and shared the singing and harmonies. It was at this stage that the songwriting partnership of Lennon and McCartney started to blossom, with songs such as "One after 909", "Hello Little Girl", "That's My Woman" and "In Spite Of All The Danger", which was on their first record. Once Paul forged his songwriting with John's, they clearly hit it off together.

Witnessing their drive and raw ambition, we all thought they would make it, but even then, who could have predicted their unprecedented international success?

One of The Quarrymen's first appearances after Paul had joined was at Wilson Hall in Garston. They played there on a number of occasions in late '57 and early '58. There is a well-known photograph, taken by the late

The Quarrymen in their bootlace ties: but where was it taken?

Leslie Kearney, of the new look Quarrymen, with John and Paul wearing white jackets and everyone wearing black, bootlace ties.

This photograph has been almost universally accepted to be at New Clubmoor Hall in Norris Green, North Liverpool. I dispute that claim. To my recollection, the photograph was taken by Leslie at Wilson Hall, Garston.

I was there on that Thursday night, as I was on a couple of others at Wilson Hall. Leslie gave to me a couple of the original prints from that appearance a few days later when we were back there at Wilson Hall.

Wilson Hall was easy to remember. It was a rough club and a meeting place for the local Garston Teddy Boys who used to brag about going there to fight their arch enemy, the Dingle gang, and anyone else who fancied their chances.

Former site of Wilson Hall, Garston

Both gangs were known to use bicycle chains, knuckle-dusters and flick knives that they obtained off Spanish sailors from the boats in Garston docks, so it was claimed. It was always best to give them a wide berth, which the Quarrymen did whenever possible. Although on one occasion and after John, as usual, had been flirting with the girls in the audience, the local Teds waited outside for the Quarrymen to leave.

When the lads came out and saw what was waiting, panic set in. A few punches were thrown and dodging their way past, The Quarrymen ran as fast as they could. Len had the tea-chest bass, which he quickly abandoned, and although I wasn't a Quarryman, I also ran with them in case the Teds thought that I was. Fortunately, tea-chests were inexpensive and readily available in those days, so Len, ever laid back, and the lads, were not too concerned.

Colin and I had a struggle keeping up, as we had to carry the drum kit between us. Colin could not afford lose his drum kit, as he was still paying it off at Frank Hessy's music shop, not far from The Cavern Club. Luckily for us, the Teds were the worse for wear as they seemed to be drunk and couldn't run too far.

John always wanted to know why he was regularly being singled out. I am sure he knew that it was most likely that, being the lead singer with a smile on his face and winking at the girls in the audiences, while attempting to emulate his rock 'n' roll heroes, wound their boyfriends up no end. Not the thing to do at Wilson Hall.

The fastest runner was John, who always had a reputation for being 'hard'. He was, without doubt, the automatic leader of The Quarrymen and perhaps a little tougher than the rest of them. A self-confessed bully, he could be quite sarcastic, sometimes making veiled threats and he was far more outspoken than the others.

The Quarrymen often had arguments amongst themselves but they rarely got heavy: they were usually just "handbags at dawn", so to speak. In sleepy Woolton Village, the young teenage lads most likely did think of John as being hard, with his Tony Curtis hairstyle, his tight jeans, his swagger and check shirt, plus his drive and raw ambition.

John was a charismatic and talented rebel, of course, but in truth and although he deliberately dressed the part, it was mostly false bravado and John always said that he was never a real Ted. He would not have been thought of as 'hard' in the tougher areas of Liverpool. He was as terrified as the rest of us that night at Wilson Hall.

The discarded tea-chest was still where it had been dropped a couple of days later and the lads retrieved it, knocked about, but still in one piece. This may well have been the Quarrymen's final visit to Wilson Hall, although I'm not too sure, but who could have blamed them if it was?

HOLYOAKE HALL: Smithdown Road, Wavertree

Holyoake Hall, near Penny Lane

Holyoake Hall, where The Quarrymen played a few times, was above the original Co-Operative store in Smithdown Road, just a block or so along from where the Dutch Café used to be. It was one of the better venues that the Quarrymen played, and apparently the ballroom had a sprung floor. There was a long flight of stairs to negotiate, which made it awkward carrying the gear in and out. Although it was not ideal, most groups were used to such situations, as there were many similar entrances that presented the same problems, the original Cavern Club, for instance.

STANLEY ABATTOIR SOCIAL CLUB:
Prescot Road, Old Swan

Stanley Abattoir in 1958, scene of their disastrous gig in '57

An unusual venue for the lads which, organised by Nigel Walley, was at the Stanley Abattoir Social Club in Old Swan, on Saturday 16th Nov. 1956.

It was a dance night for the club members and their families. The Quarrymen did not know that part of Liverpool, but I did, and I gave them directions. We were supposed to meet up at the Abattoir. (An abattoir is also known as a slaughterhouse). It was a dark night, there was a bitter wind, and after waiting around for them to show up, somebody suggested that I have a look in at the nearby pub, The Cattle Market. I had never been in this pub before and it was a bit of a rough area. I slowly opened the door and looked in, but I couldn't see the lads.

I was just about to leave when I heard a shout; "Charlie" – they were all tucked away in the far corner. "We're just having a quick one", said John, but it seemed they had already had a few 'quick ones'. "We're just calming our nerves", said Paul. "We'll be on soon," said Colin, and with that we all vacated the pub, and I didn't even have time to get a drink. The lads had clearly had enough to drink, and at their young age, it didn't take a lot to make them a little legless. The first half performance was bad, and once the alcohol started to take effect, the second half was even worse.

The crowd were not happy and they were shouting and hissing near the end. The Quarrymen made a hasty retreat, and on this occasion they certainly were not invited back!

Stanley Abattoir today

SKELLAND'S DANCE SCHOOL: Sefton Park Road

I knew of a dance school near the traffic lights at the junction of Croxteth Road and Sefton Park Road where they played Elvis, Jerry Lee, Fats Domino, Little Richard and the like during the breaks. I had been there before and I mentioned it to John and he was keen to check it out. John, like me, wasn't a dancer and we just went for the music and talent. We couldn't always get hold of the latest records, so we depended on Radio Luxembourg to hear the latest rock 'n' roll tracks from America. Trouble was, as I mentioned, the reception was very poor and Radio Luxembourg kept fading in and out. It was very frustrating, especially if you wanted to learn the words as John did. If he didn't learn all the lyrics to the complete song he would just make the missing words up.

John met me at Skelland's Dance School one evening and he was a little apprehensive about paying the 2 shillings entrance fee. I persuaded Mrs. Skelland to let him in for free as it was his first visit. Once inside, he wasn't impressed with the ballroom music, but he came to life once the rock 'n' roll music came on during the breaks. Tapping his feet and hands, John, like me, hated dancing. He thought it was a waste of energy, so he just stood against the wall checking out the local girls, while "Heartbreak Hotel" and other rock 'n' roll music blasted out. Some of the records he had never heard before, but he remarked; "the local talent isn't up to much". When we got outside, I introduced him to Norman Kuhlke of the Swinging Blue Jeans - his band were regulars at Wilson Hall in Garston - and their conversation was about all things rock 'n' roll and how much they loved it. At that time, they were both nobody in the world of pop music; little did we know how soon that would change!

ST. BARNABAS CHURCH HALL: Penny Lane, Liverpool

On a few Saturday nights in 1957, the Quarrymen played a dance at St. Barnabas Church Hall, which we called 'Barney's' . We would meet up at the Rose of Mossley pub in Rose Lane at about 7pm beforehand for a few drinks. It was a spacious pub that was always very busy on a Saturday night, and just a short walk from 'Barney's'. Colin would always have his obligatory 'black velvet', cider and Guinness, although a true black velvet was made up with expensive champagne, and cider was the substitute. Colin always blames me for introducing him to black velvet, but I can't recall ever drinking it myself. In fact, I think it was Colin who introduced me to drinking alcohol. I'm sure I was teetotal until we met! Although Colin and I were working, money was always a bit tight, and of course we always had to mug John, as he hardly ever had any money.

John usually drank mild or brown mixed, and anything else if it was free. At about 8pm, we would all head for 'Barney's', the lads all eager to get started, and me, just as eager to see them play. Mossley Hill was a quiet area in those days, and as we neared the church hall on a

Dovedale Towers, Penny Lane - the former St. Barnabas Church Hall

warm evening, the sound of ballroom music could always be heard drifting toward us from the open windows. On entering, the place was alive with sedate couples dancing a waltz or quickstep to the resident dance band.

The Quarrymen line-up varied week by week, depending on who was available at any given time, but the line up at 'Barney's' definitely included Colin, John, Paul, Rod, Len and Eric.

The Quarrymen played during the interval, which was about 20 to 30 minutes long and I can still see and hear Paul doing his Little Richard numbers, with the comical sight of the ballroom brigade jiving in all their finery.

Our favourite pub where we would be served, no questions asked

Paul's Little Richard songs were really good for such a young lad, and he certainly got everyone jiving. Those of us that stayed around until closure would make our way to the Old Dutch Café on Smithdown Road, not far from Penny Lane.

THE OLD DUTCH CAFÉ:
Smithdown Road, Liverpool.

At 'Dutchies', there was always a warm welcome from the owners Betty and Frank, and on chilly nights it was great to get inside, out of the cold air, and to get a warm drink and a pie or sausage roll. In the back, they had a long miniature skittle table that John loved to play on, plus some pin ball machines and a jukebox playing the latest music in the background.

In those days, everywhere seemed to close at around 10pm, with the exception of 'Dutchies' and a few places near to the city centre. Nobody had transport and so we rarely went into town unless it was necessary, as we would most likely end up walking home. York and Young, now a bathroom centre, occupies the premises and it is good to see that they have erected a lovely windmill replacing the old one, outside high up for all to see. Inside the shop, they have a small display with photographs and notes on the café history and the Beatles connection at 'Dutchies' – aka The Old Dutch Café.

In my search for a photo of the café, I contacted Betty and Frank's granddaughter Donna, who told me the history of the Dutch Café.

Inside the Dutch Cafe

Betty serving a customer

Her grandparents owned the café from the early '50s until 1972, when Betty became too ill to carry on, and she passed away later that year.

Frank also died a few years later. Donna's mum, Carmel, who lived above the café, told me that the family had always been upset by claims made by the late Pete Shotton in his book, when he said that he was a partner in the café.

I had a copy of 'The Beatles, Lennon and Me', but I never read it, so I dug it out to double-check what I had been told.

Apparently, Pete and John were showing an interest, and they even had the café surveyed, but nothing came of it. Betty and Frank had suggested that, if Pete was serious, he should "have a go" and work at the café for a while as a trial before he and John committed themselves.

At this suggestion, Pete accepted the offer and worked at 'Dutchies' for a few weeks, after which he disappeared and nothing materialized. Pete certainly was never a partner. The family were also upset that

Owner Betty, outside the Old Dutch Café

Pete referred to the Dutch Café as 'sleazy'.

Such a claim was totally out of order, unnecessary and untrue. Everything was clean and tidy, as can be seen in the photo (previous page) with the highly polished counter and tea urn.

I do not know why Pete said what he did about 'Dutchies', and I like to think that he must have confused the café with another from his past. The Dutch was not The Ritz, but it was a clean, warm and inviting café with a great atmosphere, and far from being sordid.

When the Beatles needed somewhere to recharge their batteries after performing in local clubs, Frank and Betty would make them most welcome, and they would even close the café so that the lads could relax and have a little privacy away from their fans. I was there late one night when the café doors had been closed and John told me that for him, 'Dutchies' was like a second home. John certainly loved the place and he mentioned it in his original draft of his song "In My Life".

York & Young, who now occupy the Dutch Cafe site

"Penny Lane is one I'm missing
Up Church Road to the clock tower
In the circle of the Abbey
I have seen some happy hours
Past the tram shed with no trams
On the 5 bus into town
Past the Dutch and St. Columbus
To the Dockers Umbrella
That they pulled down".

John Lennon

Beatle fans will understand the significance of most of the places in the draft, with the possible exception of the 'Dockers Umbrella'. Liverpudlians loved their 'Dockers Umbrella', which was demolished in 1957 because it would have been too expensive to repair.

This was the Overhead Railway that ran along the

The "Docker's Umbrella", the Liverpool Overhead Railway

Mersey Docks from Dingle in the South to Seaforth at the Northern end; about 7 miles in total. It is believed that the design originated in New York and it opened in 1893. At its peak it was used by up to 20 million passengers a year, including dock workers, until, despite public protests, its closure in 1956. The owners could not afford the necessary repairs that were needed and the "Dockers Umbrella" was dismantled in 1957.

Rosebery Street

Having checked out Pete's Dutch Café claims, I thumbed through the earlier part of his book and, to my surprise, I quickly came across more inaccuracies. According to the book, the Rosebery Street party was thrown by Colin Hanton's aunt, when, in fact it was my mother, Marjorie Roberts. Pete continues; "after performing with the Quarrymen from the back of a lorry, John and I wandered into our hostess's house, where we discovered to our delight, that beer was being made freely available to all and sundry". The story goes on about them both getting drunk, sitting on the floor surrounded by empty bottles, and so on. Pete certainly had a vivid imagination.

Pete had obviously got confused with my 21st birthday party, when the drinks were plentiful and we had so much over in the morning, we continued the party the following night. I think half of the Cavern membership were there on both nights. 84, Rosebery Street, was only a small terraced house, and we were all packed in like sardines!

IN SPITE OF ALL THE DANGER
The Quarrymen Make A Record

Plaque at 38, Kensington, where the record was made

I N EARLY SUMMER of 1958 the Quarrymen recorded "In Spite Of All The Danger/That'll Be The Day" at Percy Phillips Sound Recording Service in Kensington, Liverpool, as a demo disc. They had scraped together the money to pay for it and initially they were all very enthusiastic and excited, so everyone took it in turn taking the 78rpm record home. In *Anthology*, Paul reckoned that when we got the record, the agreement

The famous Quarrymen record

was that everyone should have it for a week each. "John had it for a week, then passed it on to me. I had it for a week and passed it on to George who had it for a week. Then Colin had it for a week and passed it on to Duff Lowe, who kept it for 23 years".

That was not quite correct, because I had it for well over two months, before I passed it back to Colin, I think. I only gave it back because I caught Sandy heating up old 78's to make plant pots from them and I rescued it just in time! By then, the interest in the record appeared to have rapidly faded. With hindsight, I was too honest for my own good!

John Duff Lowe

John Duff Lowe

Known to his friends as Duff, John Duff Lowe was a schoolfriend of Paul McCartney who was a talented pianist, brought into The Quarrymen in 1958 when the venue had a piano.

Duff told me; "I first met Paul in 1953 at the Liverpool Cathedral. Later that year, we both started Liverpool Institute Grammar School. Over the next five years we became good friends and one morning in February 1958 he said he'd joined a friend's group called The Quarrymen and asked me if I'd like to join them to play piano, which I did.

"Getting to Paul's house on the south side of Liverpool on Sunday afternoons for rehearsals, or on Saturday evening, if John or Paul had arranged a gig, which was usually over their way. It took me an hour to get there, as I lived in the Liverpool suburb of West Derby on the north eastern side of the city. I was too young to drive or own a car and so I had to travel on two buses, changing at Penny Lane. I think this, and a complaining girlfriend, was why I eventually left The Quarrymen. Also, I didn't live near enough to meet up with John and Paul during weekday evenings. I later played piano in Hobo Rick and the City Slickers, which was fronted by Ricky Tomlinson, now a well-known name in British comedy acting. Ricky jokes that I left The Beatles to join his band!"

Duff was a regular visitor to the Casbah, close to his house in West Derby. "I spent many evenings in the now famous Casbah Coffee Club, home of Pete Best. I usually went with Neil Aspinall who was a mate from the Institute and lived in the next road to me. All the Mersey bands, including The Beatles used to play at the Casbah, which was always buzzing and a great place to get away from parents.

"After leaving school I joined a firm of Liverpool stockbrokers and spent a lot of my lunch breaks at the Cavern where lunch was a hot dog and bottle of lemonade sometimes served by Cilla Black. The last time I spoke to John (Lennon) was during a break in a Beatles' lunchtime session; he introduced me to a friend, saying: 'This is Duff, he breaks stock.' This was an early Lennonism. When I went back to the Stock Exchange they would complain that I stank of disinfectant!

"After a spell on the floor of the London Stock Exchange, I decided I'd had enough of 'breaking stock' and changed course and went into banking and financial services."

Duff, of course, played on that immortal first single at Percy Phillips' Studio, as well as having it "lost" in his house for over 20 years!

However, before Duff "lost" the record, I kept taking the record to work with me. It was played every lunchtime in Littlewoods Staff Canteen in Crosby, at least twice a day for three to four weeks, in the hope that some bookings for the Quarrymen would materialise. They didn't. The only 'booking' we received was a request to perform at a party, for free, with food and drink supplied. The booking was on the outskirts of Liverpool in a place called Ford.

This is the <u>true</u> account of the party at Ford and not an inaccurate made up version as told by some authors

The Ribble Bus Station, Skelhorne Street, with the Adelphi Hotel in the background

who I have never even spoken to. I informed the lads and they were happy to go along, albeit without payment, but at least it was an opportunity to show off their talents further afield from Woolton and other local environs.

"We played mainly at fellows' parties; we'd go along with our guitars and get invited in. We either got free cokes or plates of beans; the only time we got anywhere near money was when we started entering for Skiffle competitions. We'd get through the early rounds, keeping going to try and win something".

George Harrison

It was a Friday evening when we met up and set off from Skelhorne Street (off Lime Street) on a double-decker Ribble bus. Colin put his drum kit in the luggage compartment under the stairs, but I don't recall if the tea-chest was brought along. It wouldn't have fitted under the stairs along with the other gear anyway. Everyone went up to the top deck where there were long seats with no central aisle, just one on the right. It was empty upstairs, so we had all the seats to ourselves, and after a lot of larking about, singing a few songs, with John repeating; "Are we there yet?" in one of his "Goon" type voices, we finally arrived in far flung Ford.

John loved *The Goon Show* which was aired on BBC radio in the late '50s into the early '60s and was a very popular comedy show. I don't remember seeing much of Eric who was always quiet anyway, when we all piled into the house, with Pete and John who were larking about as usual with their silly jokes, which we nearly always found entertaining. If they ever gave up The Quarrymen, they could have formed a successful comedy double act!

The place was bouncing and the first thing we did on arrival was to find the food and drink, and once we did, the idea of playing was forgotten, as the loud rock 'n' roll music blasting out from the record player seemed to keep everyone happy. As usual, Pete got stuck into the food straight away, but Colin was not happy that his favourite 'black velvet' was unavailable and so he had to make do with bottled brown ale. John was busy weighing up the girls, but he was also unhappy because they all seemed to have partners. "No spare talent – not much of a party lads," he shouted loudly over the music. Nobody seemed concerned that the group were not bothered to play, and the party was going along nicely with the early American rock 'n' roll music filling the house.

In the early hours, with the party dying down, nobody had any cigarettes left, so John and Paul decided to go down to the shops to find a cigarette machine. The smokers amongst us were all gasping for a fag and it seemed an age before John and Paul returned. What a let-down when they told us that they couldn't find a machine. "This is woolly-back country (slang for someone not from Liverpool); they probably don't know about ciggie machines out here," said John. He continued; "but look what we've got," and he proudly produced what is known in Liverpool as a "cocky watchman's" red lamp.

So called 'cocky watchmen' used to light the red lamp during dark nights to warn others of a hole in the road or similar. We all thought it was hilarious to see John waving the lamp around in front of Paul. Colin, having had his fill of bottled beer was already asleep in a chair and, eventually, we all settled down wherever we could to sleep: chairs, floor, stairs etc., until the first buses back into Liverpool town centre started running around 8am on the cold Saturday morning.

At about 7.30am, bleary eyed and tired out, everyone started heading towards the front door, eager to catch the first buses home. However, nobody could open the door. A few half-asleep people tried without success and so, eventually, we all had to leave by the back door. Once we were at the front of the house we checked the front door, and it was then obvious that cement or similar had been pushed into the mortice lock and it had set hard.

Only two people had left the house and returned in the early hours - John and Paul - who both denied any knowledge of the cement, even though they would have had access to it at the "cocky watchman's" hut. I was sure that Paul wouldn't have done it and John confirmed my suspicion with a grin in his face as he winked at me while protesting his innocence during his denial, but we all had no doubt it was him.

Everyone split up and went their own separate ways home, and John asked; "D'you wanna come down town with me to pick up me new Hofner, Charlie?" I said, "OK", believing that a Hofner was a harmonica. Colin and Pete came along with us and Pete quietly informed me that a Hofner was a guitar, and that a Hohner was a harmonica. At first I thought that was another of Pete's jokes, but Colin told me it wasn't, and confirmed what Pete had said.

I can't remember if Paul or anyone else came with us.

We caught the bus, drums and all, and went to Frank Hessy's at Whitechapel in the city centre. John's Aunt Mimi had been paying money off the guitar, and now it was finally paid for. Hessy's was one of the few shops that would accept weekly payments and the look on John's face when he finally picked up the guitar and examined it from top to bottom said it all. We left Hessy's, and John walked off with a swagger; he was like a cat with the cream, carrying his old guitar over his shoulder while strumming the new one.

We followed, carrying the drum kit between us, until we caught our bus home. I got off at Rosebery Street on Princes Avenue to go home and get some sleep in readiness for Saturday night at the Cavern. Colin, Pete and John continued their journey to Woolton Village.

On the following Monday when I returned to work at Littlewoods in Crosby, the girl that had invited us to her house party was very annoyed with me. She wanted to know why the group never played and, more importantly, asked who had cemented the front door lock and I suggested it must have been one of the other party-goers. I mean, would John ever get up to a trick like that? Would he? John had an uncanny ability to create all sorts of mischief, then successfully shift the blame elsewhere.

In the beginning, The Quarrymen would happily play wherever they could for the publicity and the experience, usually for free, and especially if there was food and drink supplied. Offering free drink was a big mistake. The lads were only young teenagers at the time, except for Colin who was a year or two older, and he was more accustomed to drinking than the rest of the lads. It didn't take much for the novice drinkers to end up drunk, so much so, that they found it difficult to carry on playing on some occasions.

It was just as bad when it came to drinking. If they were playing near Woolton Village, at the end of the night I would usually stagger along with Colin to his house nearby. Sometimes, we would take two steps forward and one step back until we finally got there, where we would both sleep it off. Otherwise I would have faced a long walk home. In the morning when we were half dead, we would sit by the gas fire and Colin's mum would make us toast and tea, which was always very welcome.

It was ironic that, when Colin was 18 and legally allowed a drink in a pub, he was often questioned about his age. He did look younger than the rest of the lads who were all truly under age, but they had no difficulty in being served alcohol.

Colin eventually started carrying a copy of his birth certificate when we were going on a booze up. Whoever looked the oldest on the night would be volunteered to get the next round in. The pubs were usually overflowing at weekends, and we used to stay out of view of the management as much as we could; in spite of all the danger!

"Young" Colin Hanton

FROM QUARRYMEN TO BEATLES
Come With Me To The Casbah

Lowlands, Haymans Green

J OHN LENNON RE-NAMED the Quarrymen a number of times before they became known as The Beatles. In the summer of 1959, John, Paul, George and Ken Brown had a residency at The Casbah Coffee Club in Haymans Green, West Derby, the home of Pete Best. It was George Harrison who had got the gig after playing at Lowlands, which is also on Haymans Green.

Lowlands is now managed by the West Derby Community Association. It is a beautiful grade 2 listed building. It could also be called the birthplace of Merseybeat: from 1958 until 1961, the basement was used for the Sundays-only venue of the Pillar Club. I

Ken Brown was a bass player and a member of the Les Stewart Quartet, with George Harrison. Ken and George left that group to join John Lennon and Paul McCartney at the Casbah. Ken briefly became a Quarryman for the residency at the Casbah Coffee Club, Haymans Green, West Derby on the 29th August, 1959.

never went to the Pillar Club, because I always went to the Cavern on Sundays, but during this time, many acts appeared there, including Gerry and the Pacemakers, The Searchers, Billy J Kramer, The Hollies and many more including George Harrison who was a regular, playing and practicing with the Les Stewart Quartet. On the upper floor above the Pillar Club was the over 21s coffee bar.

The entrance to Lowlands

The over 21s Coffee Club still survives in its original state from the 1960s. I approached the staff at Lowlands who gave me permission to take some photographs. On our arrival, we were directed up the stairs, through doors and corridors to the locked room. On entering, it was a very strange feeling to be standing there knowing the history of the room.

All of the Merseybeat groups would have used this room to have a coffee or two with all of their young, ambitious lads (including many now world-famous groups) who would wait for their turn to play all those years ago. Inside, although some items of furniture have been removed, the room has been untouched and preserved in its original state, with just the seating around the perimeter and the remnants of a counter and a hot

The over 21s club upstairs

The Over 21s Club upstairs

The now empty Over 21s Coffee Club

water urn. The only window overlooks the lovely garden and grounds. It's hard to imagine the many now famous Merseybeat groups that gathered in this room for a coffee, and to chat about what the future held for them. Little did they know what was awaiting most of them.

At the Casbah Club, the Quarrymen line-up of John Lennon, Paul McCartney, George Harrison and Ken Brown played the opening night of the club on 29th August 1959.

John and I were still friends and he was always on the lookout for new records. My record contact let me have a couple of records by Sonny Terry and Brownie McGhee who sang blues/folk music, and they were big at that time. When John found out about the records, he wanted to borrow them. I told him he could have one at a time, because he had a habit of 'forgetting' to return them.

I exchanged the first record for the second about a week later at a pre-arranged meeting with him when I met him at Penny Lane roundabout. John was really keen to hear more. He said that he had never heard of them before, but he was clearly impressed. Then I told him that they were due to appear at the Cavern, and he wanted to know when.

I told him the date, Saturday, 3rd October '59. "Got to see them," John said, and he was quite excited at the prospect. It is one of the few dates that I can remember with certainty, as it was two days before my birthday.

It was quite chilly at Penny Lane roundabout, so we headed for 'Dutchies', where we had a coffee to warm ourselves up.

John had a concerned look on his face and said; "I've just realized: I think we're at the Casbah on 3rd October." He was right; they were booked for that night, so that was the end of John's trip to the Cavern to see the blues duo: well that's what I thought. On the night when Sonny and Brownie finished their amazing set, I was talking to them in the small room at the side of the stage. It got too noisy, so we went to the back near the cloakroom when suddenly John came rushing down the stairs. "Are you going on?" he asked. "No, we just got off," they replied.

"This is a mate of mine, John," I said. Brownie, who was sweating profusely observed; "Man it's effing hot in here", and with that they went half way up the stairs to cool down in the fresher air. John was deep in conversation with them and asked; "Did you do Bony Moronie?" "No, we only do the good stuff, blues and folk," came the reply. Back then, with so many records by so many artists flooding the music scene, it was, on occasions, off the top of the head, difficult to know who had released what.

John was clearly disappointed to have missed their gig. "I've got a lift, so I'll have to get back to the Casbah, we're on soon; see you guys." The Casbah Club was not too far away by car. I often used to wonder if John ever did see Sonny and Brownie perform during his time in

"At the beginning the night went really well. We were all in a good mood – pulling George's leg and saying, "There's George's dad; where's his bus?" It was a real stage they'd put us on, with a curtain that came up and down. The curtain got stuck, so we played six numbers, not five, in our first spot. The busmen and clippies were all cheering, they really dug us.

In the interval we were told, "There's a pint for you lads over at the bar." That pint turned into two pints, then three. When we went on for the second spot, we were terrible. All pissed. The bloke from the Pavilion (cinema) never booked us. There was a row about it on the bus going home, and I thought, 'Right that's it. I'll not bother playing with them again."

Colin Hanton

the USA; I hope he did. Needless to say, I never did get my record back again.

It was shortly after this meeting in the Cavern that the name Quarrymen was dropped. Colin Hanton had left the group in early 1959 after an argument with Paul McCartney after a gig that they had played, which had been organised by George's dad. During the interval, The Quarrymen got drunk and played the second half really badly. It was a disaster.

John was now at Art College. Paul and George never attended Quarry Bank School and Ken Brown was only a stand-in. The music style had moved on from acoustic guitars, washboards and tea chests to electric guitars. The skiffle craze was over and a new sound, called Beat music, was being played.

John, Paul and George had entered a talent competition that was advertised in the local newspaper, *The Liverpool Echo*: "Mr. Star Maker", Carroll Levis. The auditions were to take place at the Liverpool Empire, with finals taking place in Manchester. The Liverpool auditions took place on 11th, 18th and 25th October. John, Paul and George entered the competition under their new name – Johnny and the Moondogs. Shortly after that, there were a number of other name changes and different band members coming and going, until, in 1960, John had settled on the name The Beatles.

The original Quarrymen had finished by 1959 and I was always proud of my connection with the group; good times and good memories. I'd created the poster advertising the Quarrymen's appearance at Rosebery Street and also the "QUARRYMEN" name on the front of Colin's bass drum. They represent the first ever publicity for the Quarrymen. John and Paul had moved

on from the original Quarrymen and the majority of us had met our future wives and settled into steady jobs. I would follow John and Paul's career with great interest through the following years. I wasn't shocked when, on 5th October (my birthday) 1962, the Beatles' debut single was released; "Love Me Do". It reached #17 in the UK chart, and #1 in the Merseyside chart.

I was never one to go overboard with my birthdays (my 21st being the exception), but the day "Love Me Do" was released was also my 23rd birthday and this one was special. It pleased me greatly that they had finally released a record and it was destined to be a hit. They had worked long and hard to achieve success and the partnership of John and Paul along with George's input, was now emerging for all to see. I was very proud that day, and still am, in the knowledge that I was once a friend of the lads in their formative years as they progressed from The Quarrymen to The Beatles.

"Love Me Do", The Beatles' first single

THE CAVERN CLUB
All Night Long

The Cavern Club membership card contained 'how to get there' info, helpful if you had spent time in the Grapes or White Star!

WHEN WE WENT to The Cavern Club, we would meet up at the Grapes and after a couple of drinks we would make our way over Mathew Street to descend into the Cavern. It was always hot and dingy, quite dark, with an overpowering smell of fruit plus condensation running down the walls and forming on the ceiling. But that didn't matter to us, it all added to the infectious atmosphere generated by the

MEMBERSHIP CARD

1961 SEASON

Ending 31st December, 1961

Sandy's highly collectible Cavern Membership card

loud music of jazz, skiffle or rock 'n' roll, depending on who was on stage at the time.

Facing the stage were rows of seats, and to the left of the arches and at the rear there was room, if you could find it, to dance. To the right there were seats and tables, which left a small amount of room for a jive. It was always so busy that it was difficult to find a clear space on the floor. I wasn't really into dancing at all, I just liked to watch the groups and, when possible, have a chat with friends in the audience. The girls were always the best dancers by far and many of the lads hardly moved. It was as if they were glued to the floor sometimes. I think there were around 20 Saturday "all-nighters" in total and Sandy and I went to most of them. There were also a couple of midweek sessions, but we didn't go to them, probably because we had work to go to the following morning.

Most of the "all-nighters" had a variety of jazz bands coming and going throughout the night and there were also the occasional Merseybeat groups plus some country groups. At the first "all-nighter", the Swinging Blue Genes were billed as the Blue Genes and a week later they became the Swinging Blue Genes. They later changed the name again to the Swinging Blue Jeans. They were very popular and they appeared at nearly every one of the all night sessions.

Although in the same business as the late Tony Booth, the original Beatles Poster artist, all of my working life, sadly I never got to meet him. His wonderful posters from the Merseybeat era are revered by Beatle fans everywhere. They conjure up

I think the Beatles only played the "all-nighters" a couple of times. I wasn't bothered about the lunchtime sessions and although the groups were great, the place used to be full of screaming girls on their lunch break from their place of work. Night time was better by far, with a mixture of fans who obviously came to see the groups, but also to dance and enjoy the music without too much screaming during performances. No doubt, the "all-night sessions" were the best of all and the atmosphere was tremendous. They were great value and to see such quality and quantity of groups would cost the earth today.

For around 10 shillings in old money (50 pence), there would be at least six groups throughout the night. As one group finished and were collecting up their equipment, the next lot would be rushing down the stairs, push through the crowd and start setting up ready for their turn. The small room at the left hand side of the stage was always crowded, with everyone getting in each other's way. The groups somehow, amid all the confusion, managed to get on stage on time trying to act all calm and collected.

Sandy and I thought the best night ever was at Christmas 1961, when the line-up included: The Remo

Old and new together, the Cavern crowd from the 1960's merged with the same spot as it is today. ©Keith Jones

Four, Gerry and the Pacemakers, The Searchers and of course The Beatles, plus two or three jazz bands whose names we cannot remember. It was well worth the walk home in the early hours, and was wonderful value; never to be repeated! In the early days on dark nights, when Mathew Street was dimly lit, the yellow light from the entrance would shine out and attract visitors like moths to candlelight. Weekends, especially Saturday nights, were always mad busy and we were usually all packed in like sardines with no room to dance.

I don't think there was a crowd limit back then, as everybody always seemed to get in. Cilla Black, ever cheerful, was a favourite with the crowd and would be working in the cloakroom. She was always eager to get on stage for one of her impromptu performances, which everyone loved. When I was 21, Cilla invited me into her cloakroom for a birthday kiss. It was an awkward situation as my girlfriend Sandy was with me, but goaded on by the lads, I accepted her offer.

When I came out of the cloakroom, Sandy had left to go home alone. I was in the dog house for a while but we soon got back together again. After all, it was only a quick peck!

At the "all-night sessions", which ended at 7am on Sunday mornings with little or no ventilation, it would often get too hot and we would have to climb the stairs and go into Mathew Street for some fresh air.

There was only one way in and the same way out at the Cavern. A steep flight of stairs led to a left turn down a couple more steps to the small signing table. Nowadays, this access, or lack of it, would be a major health and safety issue, as would the awful toilets. But this was the start of the swingin' sixties, when the music was far more important than any health hazards. The one way in and out meant that we could meet and talk to the artists before and after they went on stage. There was a small room to the left of the stage and we would often sit there talking to the band members while they were waiting their turn to go on stage.

Rory Storm and the Hurricanes were regulars and a great bunch of lads who were big favourites at the

Cavern. It is well documented that Rory spoke with a stammer, but once on stage, the stammer would vanish and he would always give a super performance. Rory and his group were as popular as The Beatles in the beginning.

When the music stopped I would sometimes chat with Ringo who, at the time, was Rory's drummer. My sister used to go out with John Starkey, a relative of Ringo's, and so we had something in common. Conversation could be extremely limited because of the loud music. We were very fortunate to have had the opportunity to be in the company of so many groups and solo artists from across Britain and the USA. On every visit we were able to meet and chat with the stars. Sandy and I cherish all the wonderful memories from our times there.

Signing in at The Cavern

Old Mother Riley at The Cavern?
Not Quite

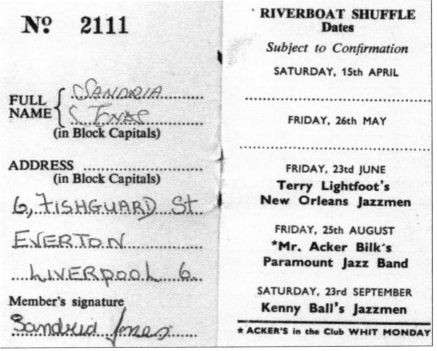

Sandy's membership card

Sandy's mum was never very happy about her staying out all night at the Cavern, but one night at around 9pm, she was in the street in front of her house, wearing her cleaning attire, when the front door blew shut. She didn't have a key, but she did have her purse. The Cavern was only a couple of miles from number 6, Fishguard Street in Everton (Paul's dad Jim was born in number 8 in July 1902), so she caught a taxi and came to the Cavern Club in her pinny, her slippers and her hair in rollers! She explained to the doorman, Paddy

Fishguard Street showing No. 6 in the foreground, Sandy's home just before it was demolished. Next door was the McCartney home No. 8 where Paul's dad, Jim, was born in 1902.

Delaney, that she needed to get the spare key off Sandy because she had locked herself out. Paddy was bemused and escorted her down the steep stairs. He knew Sandy and found her in the crowd. By the time he managed to explain over the noise what was happening, Sandy's mum was busy chatting to the clubbers who had gathered around her. "Is this where the Beatles play?" she asked.

"They're on next," someone shouted. Sandy arrived really embarrassed and quickly ushered her mother up the stairs into Mathew Street and gave her mum the spare key. "Fancy making a show of me dressed like Old Mother Riley", Sandy said. "They seem like a nice lot", her mum replied unconcerned, "so I'm not worried if you stay the night anymore", as Sandy bundled her into the taxi that had just arrived.

Sandy then sheepishly went back down the stairs, red-faced, into the Cavern. Everyone thought it was a great laugh and the incident was soon forgotten when The Beatles took to the stage. Sandy, however, never forgot.

The Beatles at The Cavern © Cavern City Tours Ltd.

Paddy Delaney
Cavern Doorman

In all our times at the Cavern we never saw any trouble inside. In the early days, a rough element of Teddy Boys had taken root and in 1959, the late Paddy Delaney, originally on the door at the Locarno, a local dance hall in nearby West Derby Road, was drafted in to sort things out. Paddy, (he didn't like to be called a bouncer) was known as the "Gentle Giant" and he knew how to handle difficult situations with the minimum of fuss. The former guardsman, in his dinner suit and cummerbund, always looked the part and the regulars treated him with great respect.

He liked Al Jolson and he would occasionally get up on stage to give his rendition of "Mammy", and George

Paddy Delaney outside The Cavern

Harrison was his greatest fan. Most members knew each other and it was a great atmosphere. Alcohol was not allowed and Paddy did not let anyone in if they appeared to be under the influence. Pass outs were available and most people would go across to the Grapes or down to the White Star. Both pubs would always be very busy. Most of us would have only one or two drinks and then head back in case we missed the

The Cavern, Mathew Street

next band. Despite Paddy's diligence, there was always someone with a bottle that they had smuggled in if we wanted another drink.

At the "all night sessions", the various groups would arrive, do their set and then move on to another club in the area. As many as six to eight groups could appear throughout the night. Back then, visitors to the Cavern were extremely fortunate to have had access to some wonderful artists for next to no money, compared to today's extortionate prices. In most clubs in and around Liverpool, and there were many, the audiences were very close to the stage, unlike today when fans have to pay huge amounts to see the performers from a distance where the stage resembles a postage stamp.

At around 3am to 4am, when it was usually quite chilly, especially coming out of the humid, sweaty cellar, the Cavern would slowly begin to empty out and the weary revellers would start making their way home. By 7am,

Typical queue eagerly waiting to be admitted to the Cavern

those who had stayed the distance would finally have to leave. The buses didn't start running until about 8am on Sundays and so many of us would have to walk home; a long way when we were tired and hungry! Of course, we were all ready to go again on Sunday night! As for Paddy, he loved his time at the Cavern and was last out when it closed in 1966.

Many famous stars would often visit Liverpool and head to the Cavern for a night out. One such star at the time was Spike Milligan, from *The Goon Show*. He visited the Cavern for the first time and he is seen dancing with a Twiggy look-a-like. Alf Geoghegan, the owner of the

Spike Milligan at The Cavern. ©Debbie Greenberg

Cavern at that time, is in the centre looking on. Spike had always wanted to visit the Cavern, and he had the opportunity when in Liverpool appearing at the Royal Court Theatre.

He wasn't disappointed, and I am sure John would have wanted to be there on the night as he was a huge Spike Milligan and Goons fan. Of course John would have been preoccupied at the time as *Sgt. Pepper* was soon to be released.

THE GRAPES and WHITE STAR PUBS

Among the pubs that we used to frequent were The Grapes and the White Star. The Grapes is over the road from the Cavern and the White Star is on the bend at the bottom of Mathew Street.

The Grapes

Both were convenient and always very busy, especially at weekends with lots of Cavern fans. There were also a number of 'scallys' (a Liverpool term for local thugs). One of their rackets was selling 'spot the ball' tickets, which were numbered.

Once they had sold their quota, they would call out the winning number, which was usually one of

The White Star Pub

their mates. It was normally crowded and very noisy and nobody would hear who had won; they were too interested in drinking and enjoying themselves.

On one occasion, a big heavy guy came up to me and thrust some money into my hand. "See you outside later", he said. I wasn't too sure what was happening, but I didn't argue. I put the money into my pocket and John said that I should use it for the next round and the others quickly agreed. I disagreed; I didn't fancy getting beaten up outside and I don't mind admitting to being a coward on this occasion.

When we eventually left the pub, there was a gang of huge guys waiting outside. "Where's the money", one said, holding out his hand. "It's here", I said nervously, as I struggled to get it out of my pocket quickly. The money was snatched from me and, to my surprise, some of it was returned. The thugs sauntered off and I was left with what I assumed was some 'hush money'.

On future trips to those pubs, we were always on the lookout for the gang and if they were in The Grapes we would go to the White Star and vice versa.

THERE ARE FACES I'LL REMEMBER
All My Life

OVER THE PASSING of time you don't realise where the years have gone and my memories of the early days of The Quarrymen will stay with me for ever. It is John who put this best in the opening verse of "In My Life":

> "There are places I remember
> All my life though some have changed
> Some forever not for better
> Some have gone and some remain
> All these places have their moments
> With lovers and friends I still can recall
> Some are dead and some are living
> In my life I've loved them all".
> *(Lennon/ McCartney)*

Eric

Eric Griffiths

It was sad news that Eric Griffiths had passed away in January 2005, which was upsetting to everyone who knew him. Eric had been ill for a long time but it was still a big shock. I always found Eric to be a nice, pleasant lad, quiet and keen to learn to improve his guitar skills. He used to spend a lot of time practising with John in preparation for the next gig.

Pete

Pete Shotton

Pete Shotton, who was John's best mate, had also been ill for a long time, but it still came as a real shock when I heard the news of his passing in March 2017. I did not know Pete that well, as he was not with the Quarrymen as long as the rest of the lads.

What I did know of him was that he was never that keen on playing in the group, but he wanted to be part of the gang. He accepted that his musical ability was limited, and quite often joked about it. Pete was loud and funny, and he loved getting up to mischief, and winding John up. There was never a dull moment when he and the lads got together.

George

George Harrison

A mutual friend, sign writer George Astbury, recalls working with George when they were employed by a famous Liverpool department store, Blacklers. Going to work with George was just part of the day, before those Hamburg nights. George worked at Blacklers as a trainee electrician and he took time off from his job to go to Hamburg. However, George was sent back home from Germany because he was under age. He came back to work at Blacklers saying "just 'til I'm old enough, then I'm going back" and not long after he was away again, with these words from his boss ringing in his ears; "If you stay here George, you'll have a job for life". George wisely didn't heed the advice!

"I was just another George who had the pleasure of travelling with him to that wonderous workplace," said Astbury. Great days!

As we all know, George Harrison went on to achieve worldwide acclaim as a Beatle and as a talented musician in his own right.

Blacklers closed in April 1988.

George Harrison sadly passed away in November 2001. Although I was in his company many times, George was always busy playing his guitar; consequently I did not get to know him that much. His ability, for someone so young, was amazing and the potential was there for all to see. Whenever I was in his company, he always seemed to be absorbed, practising on his guitar, which he took so seriously, so I was always careful not to distract him.

I remember George as a quiet, pleasant and happy young lad whose dedication proved to be so worthwhile.

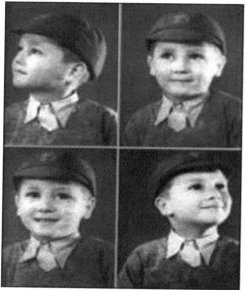
A young John Lennon

John

The biggest shock for all of us was when John died on 8th December 1980. It was Tuesday morning and I had just come downstairs to get ready for work at about 7.30am. I put the radio on and heard the news that John had been shot dead. I couldn't believe it and I was rooted to the spot for a while listening to the news, then I shouted up to Sandy; "John's dead, he's been shot".

For a moment, she thought I was mistaken, then she heard the news for herself. We were both in shock: it was like a bad dream, totally unexpected. Friends rang to ask if we had heard the news. Getting ready for work was forgotten and everything seemed as if it were in slow motion. We could not get away from the news on the radio, T.V., and in the papers.

Later, Sandy and I went to Mathew Street, where many fans milled around deeply upset and crying. The atmosphere was dreadful. John had died and so had most of Liverpool on that fateful day. One of Liverpool's favourite sons had been taken from us in such tragic circumstances.

But we are all resilient and when the mourning was over, we all took comfort in the knowledge that we still had the Beatles wonderful musical legacy.

A while after John had died, I was told that he longed for his old friends in Liverpool to contact him when he was living in New York. I never knew this and I very much regret that I never did get in touch. I always wanted to write to John at the Dakota, but decided not to, thinking that others may have thought that I was trying to cash in on his fame.

Nowadays, there is always a steady flow of fans to "Mendips" and Strawberry Field that John loved so much.

John outside Mendips

A HARD NIGHT'S DAY
The Northern Premiere

The balcony of Liverpool Town Hall where The Beatles appeared before thousands of fans

THE SUCCESS OF The Beatles took years to achieve and so many people have helped them along the way. Their achievements have been honoured in so many ways, but the one they felt most proud of was on 10th July, 1964 when Liverpool held a Civic Reception for the boys. On the day of their homecoming, the streets of Liverpool from the airport to the city centre were lined with thousands of proud Liverpudlians waving and cheering the boys as they went past in their limos.

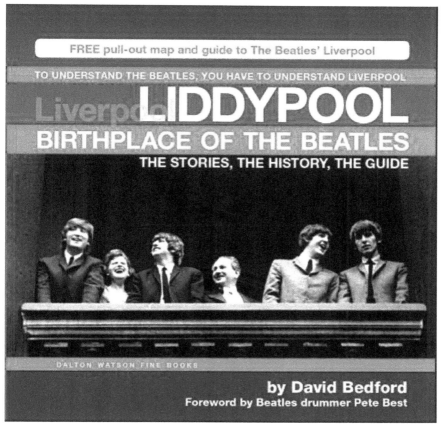

Cover of "Liddypool", showing The Beatles on the balcony of Liverpool Town Hall on 10th July 1964

After the meal at the Town Hall and making an appearance on the Town Hall balcony to the thousands of fans that had gathered outside on the streets, The Beatles made their way to the Odeon Cinema on London Road for a charity Northern premier of their new film, *A Hard Day's Night*.

Sandy worked as an usherette at the Odeon Cinema in Liverpool at the time and she was scheduled to be there

Sandy at the Odeon as an usherette

when *A Hard Day's Night* had its Liverpool premiere. It was a red carpet event and was attended by many celebrities.

There were thousands of fans outside the cinema in London Road and Sandy had difficulty gaining entrance.

The Odeon Cinema, where The Beatles premiered A Hard Day's Night. It was demolished in 2008.

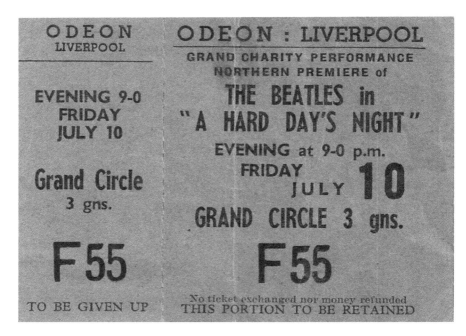

After all, how many girls would have tried to get inside the Odeon by any means? Sandy had to convince the policemen that she was genuinely an employee at the cinema and late for work. Thankfully, she was escorted by the police, through the crowds and made her way into the Odeon.

"My sister seated them, as she worked there too. When the audience were all seated, the curtains opened and The Beatles went on stage to thank everyone for turning up. The girls were screaming so loudly, you couldn't hear yourself think.

When they left the stage, a few girls managed to get backstage to catch up with them. Mr.Draycott, the Odeon's manager at the time, asked Sandy to go backstage and find the girls. She found them and

'Robbo's' wife, Sandy, showing people to their seats at the Odeon

ushered them back to the cinema and as she did, The Fab Four came along, accompanied by their wives and girlfriends.

"Hi Sandy", shouted John, then told the lads; "this is Robbo's wife". Sandy smiled and her friends envied her. However, she still had a job to do, so she and a colleague took the lads up to the circle to their seats in the front. By now, the film had started and nobody noticed them in the dark. They sat back and enjoyed the film.

The Beatles were then whisked away after the film had finished.

STRAWBERRY FIELD FOREVER

Let me take you down.....

The original Mansion at Strawberry Field

WHEN I WAS writing this book, Sandy and I were invited down to Strawberry Field to see the spacious grounds and the modern buildings that were being replaced. Much of the wooded grounds near the Vale Road wall, which John and his mates would bunk over, had already been replaced by residential housing following the demolition of the original mansion (above) at the beginning of the '70s. But even those replacement structures and the surrounding gardens had now fallen into disrepair. It was sad to see how overgrown the garden areas had become. Everywhere was taken over

The 1970s buildings at Strawberry Field

by a tangled mixture of grass, weeds and spreading bushes. I don't think John would have easily recognised the grounds of his beloved Strawberry Field in this present state. I had intended to take some photos, but there was not much to see. It was difficult to get through

Fans wait outside the famous red gates at Strawberry Field

The playground at the old Strawberry Field, where the mansion used to stand

the mass of weeds, but, after a struggle, I managed to get down to the famous red gates. I took a photo from the inside looking out onto Beaconsfield Road and, as I was about to take another, a coach load of Japanese tourists pulled up. Imagine their surprise when they saw me on the other side of the gates. They were all excited and wanted to know who I was, but it was so noisy with the building work and traffic on the road outside of the gates that they could not hear me.

I had some business cards with me, so I passed them through the gate. They all wanted one, so I gave them all that I had with me, which was about twenty. After taking their photos, they happily got back onto their coach and waved goodbye through the windows.

The good news is that the Salvation Army had been fundraising for several years to enable them to build a

The new Strawberry Field Visitor Centre

brand new visitor centre to replace the 1970s buildings that hadn't been in use since 2005. The new building and landscaped gardens are now complete and they have already become a major tourist attraction.

Strawberry Field now has a training and work-placement hub for young people with learning difficulties, covering retail, catering and gardening. There is a shop selling all sorts of souvenirs, a café which as well as an eating place, is also a great meeting place. There is an exhibition area that tells the history of John's connection with Strawberry Field and the writing of the iconic "Strawberry Fields Forever".

It is a warm and friendly place where visitors are always most welcome.

IMAGINE how happy John would have been knowing that his beloved STRAWBERRY FIELDS really will be FOREVER!

YOU SAY HELLO
I Say Goodbye

T HE LAST TIME THAT I SPOKE TO JOHN.

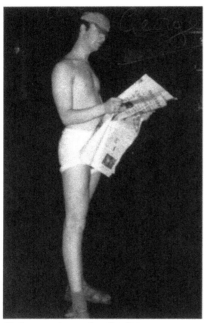

John acting the fool in Hamburg

Sometime in the early '60s, I had slipped out of work in the morning and the reason why escapes me, but it involved a bus journey. On the return trip, I sat in the front seat upstairs on the double-decker. When it was nearing my stop, I got up and made my way to the rear stairs. To my surprise, there was nobody on the top deck, except one person in the back seat.

It was John: "Alright Charlie," he shouted. "How's it going John?" I asked as I headed to the stairs. "It's okay, but I'm knackered: I've just come back from Hamburg.

"See you Charlie," he shouted, as I ran down the stairs to get off at my stop, anxious to return to work before I was missed, not realizing I would never see John again.

During the summer of 1985/86 when I was working at the Liverpool Art College, I went to collect my car from the underground car park. I noticed a large black car pulling in and two big guys got out, followed by Linda and Paul. I went over to say hello, and the minders were not too pleased, but I said; "Hi Paul, I'm Charlie". Paul looked bemused. "We were pals in the Quarrymen days", I said. Then it clicked with Paul. "Charlie", he said, shaking my hand, "it must be 30 years since we last spoke. How's things?" Paul asked, followed by; "Linda, this is Charlie". Linda was also bemused saying; "Hi Charlie, how are you doing?" It was the one and only time that I met her.

We exchanged a few more words, then Paul apologised, as he had a scheduled meeting at LIPA to attend. Most of us see Paul regularly on TV and in the media and he is instantly recognised. Paul had not seen me for a long time and I have become an "old wrinkly", now wearing specs! My once dark hair is now grey, (well, I did get married) so it's only to be expected that he did not recognise me!

I was upset when I learned that the lovely Linda had passed away in '98: she was so nice and I am very pleased to have met her.

MEETING YOKO and SEAN

My Quarrymen photos were used in the Andrew Solt film *Imagine* in 1988 and, as a consequence, Sandy and I were invited to the premiere at the Odeon, Leicester Square, in London. We were both busy working in Liverpool on the day of the premiere, so we hurried home to get ready to catch the afternoon train to London, not realising what a posh 'do' it would be. Everything was done in a rush that afternoon, as we had

Yoko's message and photo to Sandy and I

lots of pets to see to before we left for the train at Lime Street.

By the time we reached London, we were tired and hungry. Somewhere near the Odeon, we found a burger place and got something quick to eat, taking care not to drip tomato sauce onto our 'best' clothes. When we reached the Odeon, there was a huge crowd of fans and onlookers lined up either side of a long red carpet, which meant that there was only one way in.

We didn't know that we would have to walk up the red carpet in front of hundreds of fans and photographers, and it was a little daunting for us two humble Scousers. No doubt the crowd were wondering who we were. It was such a great night for us, and, as rubbing shoulders with lots of stars, we got to meet Yoko, who was very polite and petite and was accompanied by a very young Sean. I presented Yoko with one of my photographs of the Rosebery Street party and she was delighted.

Yoko later sent a nice signed photo to us both, which we have framed and on display at home.

We didn't know until it was too late that there was an after show party to which we were invited. We had made no arrangements for our animals, so we had to catch the train home to see to them.

ALL I'VE GOT IS A PHOTOGRAPH

It Reminds Me Of The Places We Used To Go

Me, proudly holding one of my photographs from Rosebery Street

ON 22ND JUNE 1957 in Rosebery Street, I was fortunate to have been loaned a camera and I took the very first photographs of John Lennon and The Quarrymen who were playing on the back of a lorry outside of my house.

Me and Sandy

The photos that I took on that borrowed Kodak Brownie remained undeveloped for a few weeks, until I read up on how to produce some prints. Having got hold of some developer and fixative, the three photos that were on one roll were printed in a makeshift dark room under the bed in my bedroom with the curtains closed. I decided to leave the second full roll of negatives for another day, when I could afford to have them developed by a professional at the local chemist.

A few years later, after Sandy and I had moved to Willis Square in Everton - and when we had some spare cash - Sandy decided to take the roll to a local chemist,

Normans in Heyworth Street, Everton, to have them developed and printed up. When she went to collect them a couple of weeks later, she was told that the negatives had been lost. We were annoyed, but accepted that they were not all that important, as they were just happy snaps of our mates.

Little did we know! The photos have never surfaced in all these years, so it seems obvious to me that they were well and truly lost. The remaining "set of three" photographs are now famous the world over, but it was a long time before any interest was shown in the photos, mainly because I never told many people about them.

Also, I never boasted about being friends with John and The Quarrymen. I think that was down to the fact that everyone and their dog in Liverpool claimed to have known the lads at the time, when what they really meant was that they had seen them many times at the Cavern or other clubs; but they certainly weren't friends.

Fans always ask me why I never took other photographs of the lads and why I didn't get their autographs. Firstly, I didn't own a camera: we didn't have a lot of money back then. I just happened to have been loaned a camera for that day of the Rosebery Street party.

Secondly, they were just a gang of unpretentious mates having fun with their group. They weren't famous. so the thought never occurred to any of us to get their autographs. As for the photographs themselves, they

One of my photos that has been expertly colourised by Tim Ware of Oakland, CA

haven't made it through the decades without incident. The first happened, many years ago, when I was naïve enough to lend copies of my photos for an exhibition, without any receipt or contract. Sometime later, when I asked for the photos to be returned, the person concerned denied that he had ever been lent them. I never got them back and I had to go to Kingston County Court, who ruled in my favour and awarded me compensation for the loss.

On another occasion in the early '90s, my original photos were starting to fade. I had six prints in total; two lots of the 'set of three' photographs. I had them valued by Sotheby's Auctioneers, who estimated them at £1,000 for each print.

At the time, I was working in Graphic Design at the Art College. I asked a lecturer colleague if he could re-photograph my six originals before they became too faded. He agreed and eventually returned the originals along with the new prints to me. I was busy at the time so I only took a quick look at the new prints, then I put them back into the large brown envelope and thanked him. He did not charge me and I was grateful for his quality work.

I had put the envelope away at home for safe keeping as we were moving house. I had no use for the photos for a couple of years, until one day when an author asked me if he could use one in his new book. It was then that I realised that one set of originals was missing. Sandy and I searched high and low for many days, until we finally gave up and accepted that they had been somehow lost. It was often on our minds over the years; did we lose them when we moved? Did we throw them out with the old newspapers? We imagined all sorts of things and it used to drive us mad.

One day back in 2016, I received a call from a Beatles fan to tell me that he was at the annual Beatles auction in Liverpool and that he saw three of my original photos auctioned off. After numerous enquiries, I found out that they had been submitted by the work colleague who had re-photographed them all those years ago. He had kept one set of the three originals behind and made the claim that he thought I did not want them.

Again, I had to go to court and, yet again, the judge found in my favour, so I was duly compensated. He was a lecturer and ran the photographic department in Graphic Design at the Liverpool School of Art and, as a professional photographer, there is no doubt in my mind that he knew full well what he was doing.

Tim Ware of Hyperarts, Oakland CA, restored my old photos for me and he did a wonderful job, considering the poor state that they were in. I did not know Tim at the time, but he and his wife Kim have since become firm friends and they stayed with us in Woolton in 2016.

My wife Sandy with our friends Kim and Tim Ware outside Mendips, 251 Menlove Avenue, John Lennon's former home.

QUARRYMEN OR QUARRY MEN?

You Know My Name

Colin Hanton's original drum kit, with "Quarrymen" as designed by me

WHILE I WAS revisiting my past and when I am invited to different venues, the one question I am often asked is about the logo on Colin's drum.

When I made the first logo for Colin's drum, I realized that one word would mean that the lettering would be too small. I wrote it as "QUARRY MEN" in two lines, so that it would be bold and easily seen. Ever since, for sixty years, fans have asked; "Is it QUARRYMEN or QUARRY MEN?"

The definitive answer is the former, and it should always be one word, just as the Quarrymen originally intended. Eventually, when the wording became damaged through wear and tear, Colin made another in the same style. I hold my hand up and admit that the confusion is down to me, but it was necessary for maximum publicity at the time. The derivation of the name has always been understood to have come from Quarry Bank School.

Nigel Walley, The Quarrymen's first manager, with Rod Davis

QUARRY BANK SCHOOL, LIVERPOOL.

EX HOC METALLO VIRTUTEM.

THE SONG OF THE QUARRY.

Words by
R. F. BAILEY.

Music by
D. SCOTT.

Quar - ry men old be - fore our birth   Strain - ing each mus - cle and sin - ew

Toil - ing to - geth - er,   Mo - ther Earth   Con - quered the Rock that was in you.

Say men the quar - ry - ing   all is done?   Read - i - ly we'll re - fute 'em

Copyright 1924.

The Quarry Bank School song shows "Quarrymen" as one word.

This assumption is not always correct and the name was definitely an amalgamation of both Quarry Bank and Woolton Quarry. Rod, Colin and Len agree with me that these two factors spawned the name Quarrymen - one word!

"Our name was inspired by a reference in the lyric in the official song of the school (Quarry Bank Grammar School) that the five original band members attended. This lyric includes this couplet that contains "Quarrymen" clearly spelled as one word, so naming the group after a word in the school song was a tongue-in-cheek reference to what some of the members felt was pompous doggerel.

The band members therefore regarded their band name as being one word, but it certainly wasn't a crucial matter in 1956! Our drummer Colin Hanton wanted to write the band name across the front of his bass drum. But there was insufficient space to write it as one word".

Rod Davis, The Quarrymen.

Rod Davis, The Quarrymen's historian

THE BEATLES' LEGACY
In The Town Where They Were Born

THE BEATLES LEGACY in Liverpool was always overlooked, particularly after the original Cavern was demolished in 1973 to make way for the new Merseyrail underground Loop Line.

The following year, a statue by Liverpool sculptor Arthur Dooley was unveiled on Mathew Street dedicated to The Beatles. The sculpture, situated across the street from The Cavern, though you have to look up or you will miss it. The sculpture was of The Madonna

holding four "cherub" babies, though when Paul's cherub disappeared, Bob Wooler mused that "Paul's cherub had taken 'Wings' and flown." A new cherub with wings did appear, but that too has gone.

Above the statue is a street sign called "Beatle Street", with another sign below the Madonna; "Four Lads Who Shook The World".

The Arthur Dooley Statue, 1974

The car park on Mathew Street before they excavated the site to create Cavern Walks and the new Cavern Club.

Fans from around the world would visit Mathew Street on their Beatles pilgrimage in search of the original Cavern, only to be disappointed. A local Beatles fan, Jim Hughes, together with his wife Liz, decided to address the issue by opening a shop in North John Street, at the top of Mathew Street, for Beatles fans to meet, calling the shop The Magical Mystery Store.

Later, Jim and Liz moved the shop to Mathew Street, which became a fan-based meeting place. In 1977, they organised the first Liverpool Beatles Convention held at The Royal Court Theatre, opposite the magnificent St. George's Hall. Cavern Mecca moved into the newly opened Cavern Walks until Cavern Mecca closed in 1984.

The dove of peace, designed by Cynthia Lennon

Cavern Walks was designed in 1982, following the senseless murder of John in December 1980 in New York. The designer was Liverpool born David Backhouse. The excavation for the site started in 1981, when they uncovered the original foundations of the Cavern, so they decided to include a new Cavern on the site.

The architects and designers were sympathetic to the legacy of The Cavern, creating the new club from thousands of the original bricks. They also asked

Cynthia Lennon to design the terracotta tiles that line the outside of the building and there is also a Rose and a Dove in honour of John's passion for peace. Inside Cavern Walks, there is a statue of The Beatles on display occupying the ground floor, which was commissioned by The Royal Life Insurance, and designed by sculptor John Doubleday. It was unveiled by Mike McCartney in the spring of 1984.

With the regeneration of Mathew Street, The Beatles' legacy was at the forefront in 1984. The Beatles Shop opened its doors at 31, Mathew Street: above the shop doorway is another statue to The Beatles. This claims

The first Beatles statues in Liverpool

174

to be the first statue of The Beatles in Liverpool. On the right of the door of The Beatles Shop it reads:

FROM US TO YOU. This, the first Beatles statue in Liverpool, has been funded by Beatles fans from all over the world and supported by the Beatles shop. This tribute to the world's greatest group was sculpted by Liverpool artist David Hughes.

In April 1984, Beatle City opened in Seel Street and was billed as The World's First Permanent Beatles

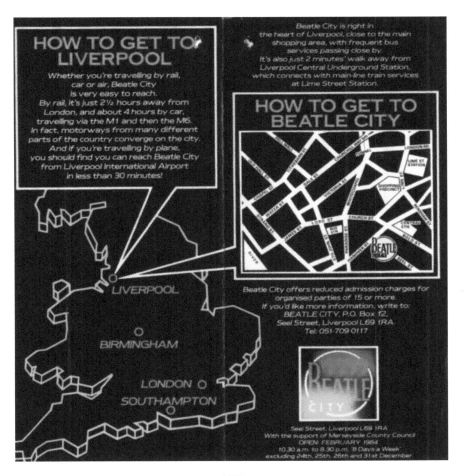

A Brief Guide To The Exhibits Displayed In Beatle City.

IN MY LIVERPOOL HOME

Views of the Mersey and liverpool in the early 1960s including the 'Brittanic', Isle of Mann ferry, 'Empress of Canada', and the Liverpool landing stage (Merseyside County Museums).

ROCK 'N' ROLL MUSIC

Model of Liverpool c. 1959. A Liverpool front room furnished with John Lennon's radiogramme. Picture of Agnes Flannery, mother of Joe Flannery friend of the Beatles, (Flannery family) and one of the reputed origins of the Beatle haircut.

Display of early contracts , letters and a hand bill relating to the engagement of groups including the Silver Beatles and Gene Vincent. (Alan Williams). Sign from above the Jacaranda coffee bar (Alan Williams).

EARLY BEATLE DAYS

Dispaly of early photographs, including John Lennon with Quarrymen in 1959 (Charles Roberts) and Paul and John in the Casbah (Cavern Mecca) Three early posters advertising the Beatles and other Liverpool groups.

HAMBURG

Letter from Stuart Sutcliffe to his sister Pauline, in which he describes and sketches stage suits done by Astrid.
Two paintings done by Stuart Sutcliffe: A Nude (Allan Williams). An abstract (George and Brenda Moore)
Double image photograph of Stu (Astrid Kercherr). Photograph of Stu and John on the beach (Astrid Kircherr).

CAVERN

Pictures of the Beatles in the Cavern with Pete Best on drums (Cavern Mecca) Display stand showing early photographs of the Beatles particularly George Harrison.
Display of Cavern microphones c. 1962, Cavern Club. Membership card (Charles Roberts) and magazine.

Display including Christmas cards, a publicity photograph of Billy J. Kramer and a handbill hand written on reverse by Paul McCartney giving his name and address in Hamburg.
Photograph of John Lennon and George Harrison receiving guitars from Mr. J. Rushw 1962 (Rushworths).
The visitors book from the re-opening of the Cavern 'second time around' 1967.

GETTING BETTER STUDIO

Studio equipment c. 1960. (John Ransom).
Studio floor includes: George Harrison's Getsch guitar used between 1962 - 1964. John Lennon's stage jacket c. 1964.
Paul McCartney's drum kit, c. 1963.

The Beatle City flyer showing some exhibition memorabilia

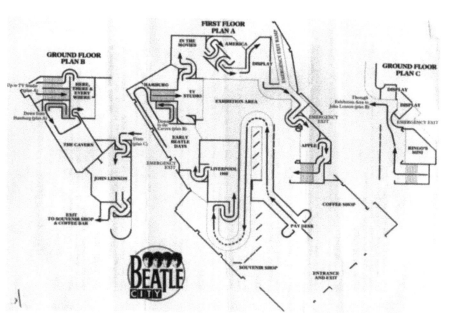

Memorabilia from Beatle City

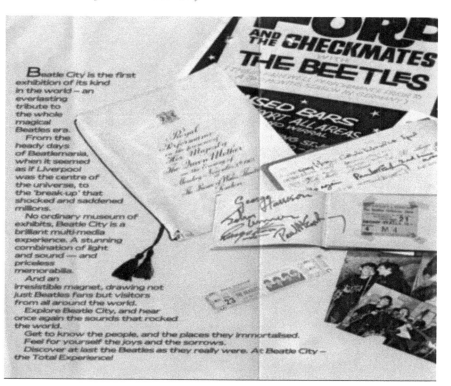

Exhibition. I had loaned my photos, with a proper agreement in place. Many other items were loaned by Beatle fans, all for free. We were all confident that our property was in safe hands, until one day the 'permanent exhibition' was no longer permanent! After three years, Beatle City closed in 1987. No notice was served and without the permission of the lenders, the exhibition was shipped to Dallas, Texas, in the States. From all accounts, there was no inventory made and I was informed that over in Dallas, people were helping themselves to some of the loan items.

Mike Byrne who was in Dallas at the time, managed to save my photos and return them to me. It was Mike, along with his wife Bernie, who later created the marvellous Beatles Story at Albert Dock.

Entrance to the Beatles Story

LIVERPOOL'S NEWEST VISITOR ATTRACTION

A MAGICAL

THE

BEATLES

Story

EXPERIENCE

A TRIBUTE TO THE WORLD'S GREATEST POP GROUP

JOHN, PAUL, GEORGE & RINGO

Albert Dock, Liverpool

The Fascinating Story of The Beatles

Join the lads from Liverpool on a Magical History Tour through the sights and sounds of the 60s
Take a trip to Hamburg. Feel the Cavern beat. Tune into flower power. THE ATMOSPHERE IS ELECTRIC!

OPEN 7 DAYS A WEEK 10am-6pm
(Hours may be extended during Summer months)
Enquiries to The Beatles Story Ltd, Britannia Vaults, Albert Dock, Liverpool L3 4AA
Telephone 051 709 1963
In conjuction with Wembley Stadium Limited. Supported by The English Tourist Board.

Flyer from the "new" Beatles Story

The Yellow Submarine exhibit at the Beatles Story

Replica of the Cavern Club inside The Beatles Story

Replica of the Cavern Club stage

Left, Bernie and right Mike at the Beatles Story opening May 1990

Mike and Bernie sacrificed an awful lot of time and money to realize their dream. Sandy and I visited on occasions, sometimes after midnight, when Mike and Bernie were still working into the early hours, constructing the exhibition.

It was a very stressful time for them, and although they are no longer involved, they have left a wonderful legacy for Beatles fans from all over the world to enjoy. Since The Beatles Story opened in 1990, more and more tourists are visiting the city each year and, unlike the early 1970s, the private sector, the pubs and clubs, tour guides, tour buses and hotels, are catering for the tourists.

The Statue of Cilla Black in Mathew Street

In 1995, The National Trust of England bought 20, Forthlin Road, the former home of Paul McCartney and restored the home with the help of Mike McCartney to the way it was in the 1960s, when the McCartneys lived there.

In March 2002, Yoko Ono bought John Lennon's house 251, Menlove Avenue, known as "Mendips". Yoko Ono

donated the house to The National Trust. The Trust restored the house to the 1950s-style, and both homes are open to view by The National Trust.

On the 16th January 2017, to celebrate the 60th Anniversary of the Cavern Club a statue of Cilla Black, who passed away on the 1st August 2015, was unveiled.

Statue of John Lennon, based on Jurgen Vollmer's photograph of John in Hamburg

The sculptor was Andrew Edwards who designed The Beatles at the Pier Head and it was funded by her sons, Robert, Ben and Jack Willis.

There is another statue in Mathew Street. It was unveiled on the 16th January 1997 for the 40th anniversary of the Cavern, and it is of John Lennon leaning against a wall and is opposite the Cavern.

The design is modelled on Jurgen Vollmer's 1961 photograph of John and The Beatles in Hamburg, which John used for his 1975 album *John Lennon Rock 'n' Roll*. At the Pier Head there is now a wonderful statue of The Beatles, which was funded by The Cavern Club, it was sculpted by Andrew Edwards and unveiled by John's sister Julia Baird on the 4th December 2015.

It has rapidly become a major tourist attraction for Beatle fans.

The new Beatles Statues at the Pier Head

COME TOGETHER

The Quarrymen Get Back Together

1997 was a special year for The Quarrymen; it was the year the remaining Quarrymen re-formed.

The Quarrymen back together in 2017. John Duff Lowe, Chas Newby, Julia Baird speaking, Colin Hanton (behind Julia), Len Garry, Rod Davis and Nigel Walley

A<small>FTER SO LONG</small> in the wilderness, it was really great to hear the news that the four remaining original Quarrymen, Colin, Len, Eric and Rod, were getting back together in 1997.

Since they re-formed for the 40th anniversary of the day John met Paul, they have been kept busy and they are as popular as ever. They have since performed at the

A skiffle group recreate the day John met Paul in St. Peter's Field

50th and 60th celebrations and they are performing better than ever: after all, they have been at it for over 60 years!

The lads have travelled the world during the last 20 years or so and their show is still a good mixture of the popular skiffle numbers and good old rock 'n' roll. Len sings the Elvis numbers with great zest and he is ably supported by Rod, Colin and Chas Newby, or should that be "Newboy"?

We are all in our late '70s now, but Sandy and I are still able to meet up with the lads quite often: we met up recently at the 60th Anniversary on Thursday 6th July 2017.

It was a lovely sunny day and the lads set off on the back of the wagon, as they did all those years ago.

They travelled down through the village, then took a left at the baths and headed toward Kings Drive, opposite Rod's old house and near Colin's old house. They turned back to eventually return up Church Road, where they took a left turn up the path that led to the church field.

There were crowds everywhere and it was noisy: the Quarrymen were playing throughout the trip. But the noise from the excited crowds and the church bells nearly drowned them out at this point. The wagon was going very slowly and I was able to walk alongside and chat to Colin some of the way. I didn't see it, but Julia Baird, John Lennon's half-sister, crowned the Rose Queen.

There were many stalls on the church field, some with games I had not seen since I was a child, and the Salvation Army band was there also. Mid-afternoon, Johnny Storm and the T-Cups, who I had never seen before, performed some great rock 'n roll numbers. The Quarrymen followed them and played many of the numbers as they had in 1957.

As usual they went down a storm with their fans shouting for more. They were followed by The Coburn Brothers and, again, I hadn't seen them before: Sandy

Len Garry at the recording session

Chas Newby, Len Garry, Colin Hanton and Rod Davis recording their latest CD in March 2020

Sandy with Yoko Kaji at St. Peter's Church, Woolton Church Hall 2017

never did let me go out much! They did a John and Paul set and were terrific. Most recently, in March 2020, we met up for a recording session and the Quarrymen were on great form as usual.

Fans had travelled from all over the world to be there on the 60th anniversary, to be part of the celebration of the day John met Paul. Inside St. Peter's Church Hall, there were press, radio and television crews; stalls selling memorabilia, souvenirs and original art work to commemorate the day, including a set of tapestries designed and made by Japanese artist Yoko Kaji.

Yoko brought a set of beautiful hand woven large

tapestries for the Quarrymen's 60th anniversary celebrations. The tapestries were hung around the walls of St. Peter's Church Hall and the display created a lot of interest and admiration for Yoko's labour of love.

In the evening, we went to the dance, although it was too crowded to do any dancing and I was rather pleased about that (my bad knee). It was a super night, with the Quarrymen doing a mixture of skiffle and rock 'n' roll.

They were followed by a very old friend (he's not that old!) Mike Byrne and his band The Sunrockers. Mike, a great versatile musician, appeared at the Cavern in the early '60s and was a member of the Roadrunners, plus a number of other groups up to the present day, as well as setting up The Beatles Story.

If you like Jerry Lee Lewis, as we do, you would love Mike's show. The highlight of the evening was when the Quarrymen, with John Duff Lowe, Chas Newby and including Nigel Walley, joined Mike on stage for a long and rousing finale that would have gone on for longer, but for the 11pm curfew at the church hall. Nigel, who was the Quarrymen's manager in the early days for a short while, was clearly in his element when he had the opportunity to play the tea chest bass.

Each anniversary day has been an uncanny replica of the 1957 original and the lads have, with a little help from their friends, been rockin' all over the world ever since they got back together.

I was chatting to new band-member Chas Newby and he told me his story of playing with The Beatles.

From The Beatles to The Quarrymen

Chas kindly sent me the following letter for publication in my book;

"The first time that I saw the Quarrymen was late August 1959 at the opening of the Casbah Club, owned and run by Mrs. Mona Best, Pete's mother. At that time, the band comprised John, Paul, George and Ken Brown. George and Ken I had seen before as part of the Les Stewart band playing at the Lowlands Club, also in Haymans Green, West Derby, but this was the first time

Chas Newby, former Beatles bass player

I had come across John and Paul. I was at school with Pete at the Collegiate, and we were all there for the opening night. Some time in October 1959, Ken Brown left the band, and I suspect the name Quarrymen was lost until Rod Davis reformed the original band in the 1990's.

Ken asked Pete to be part of a new band and Pete suggested that myself and Bill Barlow, also from the Collegiate, would be interested. Thus, the Blackjacks were born. We played at the Casbah until April 1960. As part of my further education, I relocated to Harlow, Essex. Bill was also preparing to study in Brighton, and Ken's family were moving down to the London area, so the Blackjacks folded. Thus, when The Beatles needed a permanent drummer for their first trip to Hamburg, they knew Pete was available. By this time, Stuart Sutcliffe was part of the Beatles playing bass guitar. Whilst in Germany, Stuart met up with Astrid Kirchherr and when the band returned to Liverpool in December 1960, Stuart decided to spend the Christmas period as a guest of Astrid's family.

The Beatles were now looking to establish themselves in Liverpool, but first they needed gigs and a temporary bass player to fill in for Stuart. I was back home for the Christmas vacation and Pete suggested to the others that I could fill the role until Stuart's expected return in early 1961. So, during the Christmas period, I played four gigs with The Beatles; two at the Casbah Club, one at the Grosvenor in Wallasey, and the defining gig at the Litherland Town Hall.

Len, Colin, Pete, Rod and Eric.

At the beginning of January, I was back at College and my brief career with the Beatles was over. My time with the band didn't become public until Pete produced his first book in 1985 and Mark Lewisohn's book shortly after.

In August 2013, I was at the Casbah during Beatleweek and the Quarrymen were playing. I got chatting to Rod and we exchanged telephone numbers and email addresses. He called me in 2016 to play a gig in London to celebrate Beatles biographer Hunter Davis' eightieth birthday, and I've been part of the band since then. "It's such a blast to be playing the music that was so important to us during our formative years."

Chas, second left, with The Quarrymen on stage with the Beatmasters at the Liverpool Philharmonic Hall 2018

*L-R Nick Arnott, Phil Orme, Colin Hanton, Len Garry,Martin Taylor,
Chas Newby, Mike Byrne, Rod Davis and compère Tony Ravel*

The Quarrymen also play many charity events, one was
in January 2018, when I was invited to attend Liverpool
Philharmonic Hall, on stage with The Quarrymen were
The Beatmasters (above).

*The Quarrymen re-union in 2017,
L-R – Rod Davis, Len Garry, Nigel Walley, Chas Newby, Colin
Hanton and John Duff Lowe, "Still Rockin' All Over The World"*

As for Sandy and I, it has been:

'Just like starting over.'

Own a Piece of Beatles History

You can purchase your own copy of each of my three Quarrymen photographs, signed by members of The Quarrymen and me.

Available as 10" x 8" and 14" x 11"

Also available with John colourized.

A reproduction of the original poster from Rosebery Street, A3, signed by me.

Also available, several Black or White T-shirts with The Quarrymen on.

For prices and more information, email me at diondee321@sky.com

CPSIA information can be obtained
at www.ICGtesting.com
Printed in the USA
BVHW091437111220
595376BV00016B/995